THE

APHORISMS OF ŚÁNDILYA

WITH THE

COMMENTARY OF SWAPNEŚWARA

OR

THE HINDU DOCTRINE OF FAITH

Elibron Classics
www.elibron.com

Elibron Classics series.

ISBN 1-4212-7215-6 (paperback)
ISBN 1-4212-7214-8 (hardcover)

This Elibron Classics Replica Edition is an unabridged facsimile of the edition published in 1878 by Asiatic Society of Bengal, Calcutta.

BIBLIOTHECA INDICA:

A

COLLECTION OF ORIENTAL WORKS

PUBLISHED BY THE

ASIATIC SOCIETY OF BENGAL.

New Series, No. 409.

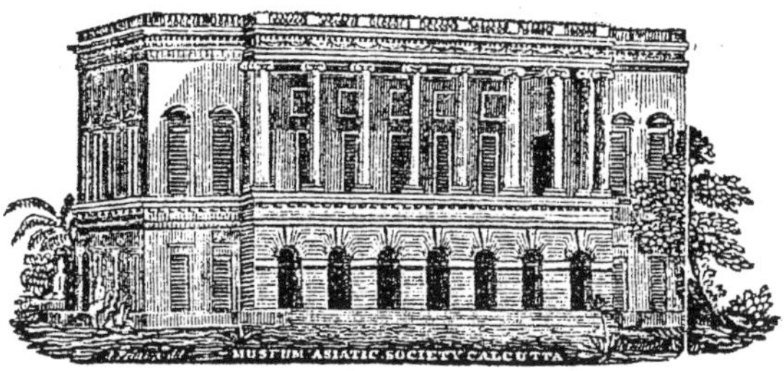

THE

APHORISMS OF S'A'NDILYA,

WITH THE

COMMENTARY OF SWAPNES'WARA,

OR

THE HINDU DOCTRINE OF FAITH.

TRANSLATED BY

E. B. COWELL, M. A.,

FELLOW OF CORPUS CHRISTI COLLEGE, AND PROFESSOR OF SANSKRIT IN THE UNIVERSITY OF CAMBRIDGE; AND HONORARY LL. D. OF THE UNIVERSITY OF EDINBURGH.

CALCUTTA:

PRINTED BY G. H. ROUSE, BAPTIST MISSION PRESS.

1878.

BIBLIOTHECA INDICA;
A
COLLECTION OF ORIENTAL WORKS
PUBLISHED UNDER THE SUPERINTENDENCE OF THE
ASIATIC SOCIETY OF BENGAL.
NEW SERIES.

THE

APHORISMS OF ŚÁNDILYA,

WITH THE

COMMENTARY OF SWAPNEŚWARA,

OR,

THE HINDU DOCTRINE OF FAITH.

TRANSLATED BY

E. B. COWELL, M.A.,

FELLOW OF CORPUS CHRISTI COLLEGE, AND PROFESSOR OF SANSKRIT IN THE UNIVERSITY OF CAMBRIDGE; AND HONORARY LL.D. OF THE UNIVERSITY OF EDINBURGH.

CALCUTTA:
ASIATIC SOCIETY OF BENGAL.
1878.

HERTFORD:
PRINTED BY STEPHEN AUSTIN AND SONS.

PREFACE.

Colebrooke, in his account of the Páñcharátras or Bhágavatas,[1] says that "a passage quoted by Śaṃkara A'chárya in his Commentary on the Vedánta Sútras (ii. 2. 45), seems to intimate that the promulgator of the Páñcharátra system was Śáṇḍilya, who was dissatisfied with the Vedas, not finding in them a prompt and sufficient way of supreme excellence (*para-śreyas*) and final beatitude; and therefore he had recourse to this *śástra*." This however is not the work translated in the following pages, as the doctrines impugned by Śaṃkara do not agree with those of the present work; nor does it contain the passage quoted by him, or that quoted by Govindánanda in his gloss, which declares that one syllable of a tantra is superior to the four vedas. Dr. Hall, in a note to his edition of Wilson's translation of the Vishṇu Puráṇa,[2] quotes some lines from Nágeśabhaṭṭa's gloss (the *Guruvyákhyá*) on Govardhana's *Saptaśati*, which condemn as repugnant to the Veda the doctrines of the Páñcharátras, the Bhágavatas, the Bauddhas, the Daigambaras, the Lokáyatas, etc.; and he adds that these verses are preceded by a denunciation of Śáṇḍilya as heretical. This may very probably refer to the supposed author of these aphorisms; but this allusion does not carry us very far back, as Nágeśabhaṭṭa

[1] *Essays*, vol. i. p. 438.

[2] Vol. v. p. 379.

was contemporary with Jayasiṃha, Rája of Jaipúr, who lived in the beginning of the eighteenth century.[1]

The name Śáṇḍilya is found in a well-known passage of the Chhándogya Upanishad (iii. 14), which recurs with a few verbal differences in the Śatapatha Bráhmaṇa (x. 6. 3); the sage is there represented as declaring that the soul within us is Brahman. His doctrine is directly referred to in Aphorism 31 of the present work, and the Commentary quotes the passage from the Chhándogya Upanishad. This doctrine is called the Śáṇḍilya-vidyá in the Vedánta-sára, and it is there characterised as consisting of devotional meditations directed towards Brahman viewed as possessed of qualities rather than as the Absolute. The author of these aphorisms apparently accepts his view as the true one, and contrasts it with those of Káśyapa and Bádaráyaṇa (cf. Aph. 29-32), the former of whom is represented as holding that Brahman is other than the individual soul, while the latter holds that the soul is nothing but Brahman, its apparent individuality being only an illusion. But the Śáṇḍilya-vidyá after all very imperfectly corresponds to the doctrine of the Śáṇḍilya sútras, which are properly a Mímáṃsá of faith (*bhakti*), as distinguished from the *púrva-mímáṃsá* which treats of ceremonial works, and the *uttara-mímáṃsá* which treats of knowledge. Their peculiar tenet is that liberation can only be produced by faith. The mundane existence of the individual soul has arisen from the want of faith, not from the want of knowledge; and faith alone can abolish it. Faith effects this by abolishing the internal organ, which is associated with the soul and disguises its real nature. Knowledge is only useful inasmuch as it removes the mind's foulness,

1 Hall's Preface to his edition of the *Sáṅkhyasára*, p. 37 *note*.

which consists of unbelief; it thus leads to faith, and this to liberation. Śaṃkara's view of knowledge is clearly expressed in the following passage of his Commentary on the Śwetáśwatara Upanishad, which will serve to bring the two views into sharp contrast. "When men, disregarding the fruit, perform works only for the sake of Íśwara, these works become indirectly a means to liberation, as being a means for producing that purity of the internal organ which is a means to knowledge, which is the means to liberation."[1]

The Bádaráyaṇa mentioned above is of course the author of the Vedánta sútras, but I am not certain about Káśyapa. There is no celebrated Vedantist teacher of that name; and it is therefore probably intended as an allusion to Kaṇáda's school. Kaṇáda is so called in the *Trikáṇḍaśesha* and in Śaṃkaramiśra's *Upaskára*, pp. 160, 161; and the Vaiśeshika school, like the Nyáya, generally holds that individual souls are infinite in number and distinct from the Supreme Being.[2] The doctrine itself, if taken as a branch of the Vedánta, very much resembles that of Rámánuja, who flourished in the first half of the twelfth century; but, though I know of no positive grounds for assigning to these Aphorisms an earlier date than the thirteenth century, I should certainly be inclined to allow them a somewhat higher antiquity.

Still the absence of all direct allusion to these Aphorisms in mediæval Hindu writers proves that they must be comparatively modern. They are the work of some anonymous teacher, who ascribed his doctrine to the ancient ṛishi Śáṇḍilya,

[1] यदा पुनः फलनिरपेक्षमीश्वरार्थं कर्मानुतिष्ठन्ति तदा मोक्षसाधनज्ञानसाधनान्तःकरणशुद्धिसाधनपारंपर्येण मोक्षसाधनं भवति। (Bibl. Indica edit. p. 254.)

[2] Cf. the Commentaries on the Vaiśeshika Sútras, ii. 1. 18 and iii. 2. 19, 20.

partly because he wished to conceal its modern origin under a name belonging to Vedic times, and also because the *Śáṇḍilya-vidyá* supplied a convenient vantage-ground for his main doctrine of the necessity of faith. He bases his doctrine on the Bhagavad-gítá, which he mentions by name in Aph. 83, and evidently quotes in Aph. 84; he applies to it the word *śabda* in Aph. 22, and the later commentator does not hesitate in several places to call it *śruti*.

The original text of the Aphorisms, with Swapneśwara's Commentary,[1] was edited by Dr. Ballantyne in 1861 in the Bibliotheca Indica. He had intended also to publish a translation, but this project was never carried into effect. Just before he left India, he had a fragment of his intended translation set up in type, containing the greater part of the first four pages; but it was never revised nor struck off. I have borrowed some of his phrases and notes in the commencement of the present translation; and I have also found assistance from some of the notes written in his MS. of the text now in the India Office Library (No. 8) in London. These notes end abruptly at Aphorism 31.

I have endeavoured to make my translation as faithful as I could; but I have not hesitated to insert between brackets those missing links which Hindu writers so often presuppose that their readers will supply, and which are generally in-

[1] Swapneśwara was a native of Bengal (*Gauḍa*), and he quotes the Gauḍa recension of the S'akuntalá in his commentary on Aph. 6; but I know nothing as to his date. There is a MS. in the Calcutta Sanskrit College Library of another Commentary by Bhavadeva, which must be considerably posterior to that by Swapneśwara, as it not unfrequently takes a line of his commentary and treats it as an original aphorism, just as we sometimes find the modern Nyáya writers do with regard to the ancient commentaries on the Nyáya sútras (see Colebrooke, *Essays*, vol. i. p. 283). Thus in p. 71, l. 6, he takes as a sútra the passage *tasya bhagavattosharosharúpasyápi layaḥ kálát pralayasámagríto vá.* He also omits certain sútras, treating them as part of the original Commentary.

dispensable to the correct understanding of the argument. I am too deeply sensible of the difficulties of Hindu philosophy to hope that I have always caught my author's meaning. Hindu philosophy, like Aristotle's works, has everywhere pitfalls for the unsuspecting reader, often hidden under some apparently simple expression; and I have no doubt fallen into some of these unawares. My translation would certainly have been better, if I had been still residing in India and had been able to consult, as I used to do, the Paṇḍits of the Calcutta Sanskrit College. I would here, however, gratefully acknowledge the considerable assistance which I have received in many difficulties, more especially in the third Chapter, from my old friend and teacher Paṇḍit Maheśa Chandra Nyáyaratna. He kindly sent me by letter explanations in Sanskrit of several passages which puzzled me; and some of these I have translated at length in the notes to my translation. He also sent me many various readings from a good MS. in the Sanskrit College Library, some of which have been of great use for correcting the printed text.[1]

One of the chief points of interest in the *Śáṇḍilya sútras* is their relation to the history of the Hindu doctrine of faith (*bhakti*). This doctrine, originally propounded in the Bhagavad-gítá and subsequently developed in the Puráṇas and especially in the Bhágavata, has become a widely spread tenet of mediæval and modern Hinduism; and the Śáṇḍilya sútras are no doubt one of the many offshoots of the theory. The date and history of its origin in India are at present unknown, and, in the general absence of historical data in Hindu literature, we may well fear that they will always remain so.

[1] I have also used a thin paper transcript of the MS. in the Bodleian Library, lent to me by Professor Max Müller.

Dr. Lorinser, Prof. Lassen, and Prof. Weber have maintained that the doctrine of *bhakti* arose in India as a more or less direct reflexion of Christian ideas; but strong objections have been urged by Dr. Muir, in the preface to his "Religious and Moral Sentiments from Sanskrit Writers," and by Paṇḍit Káśináth Trimbak Telang in the preface to his excellent translation of the Bhagavad-gítá. I cannot pretend to speak positively on the controversy; I would only confess to a somewhat hesitating inclination towards Prof. Weber's moderate opinions on the question. The idea expressed by the phrase *πιστεύειν εἰς τὸν Θεόν* is peculiarly associated with Christianity; and *bhakti*, as distinguished from the older *śraddhá*, appears, so far as we can trace it, to have risen suddenly on the Hindu horizon; but it is possible that it may have been, like so many other great conceptions, a natural product of the isolated activity of the Hindu mind. Anyhow, it is deeply interesting to trace the parallel; for the reader can hardly find a more striking commentary on Śáṇḍilya's *bhakti* than those words of Augustine, whether we view their likeness or their difference, "quid est credere in Deum? credendo amare, credendo diligere, credendo in eum ire, et ejus membris incorporari."

E. B. COWELL.

CAMBRIDGE, *Aug*. 10, 1878.

THE APHORISMS OF ŚÁṆḌILYA.

FIRST CHAPTER.

VICTORIOUS IS THE SUPREME LORD.

A COMMENTARY on the hundred Aphorisms of Śáṇḍilya is now uttered by Paṇḍit Swapneśwara, in reliance on the supreme deity; great is the marvel of the wine of Govinda's two feet, which whoso drinks does not become bewildered, while those who drink not do!

It will be declared hereafter that Liberation is the soul's reaching the state of Brahman. And as souls are absolutely identical with Brahman, their mundane condition is not natural to them, but is caused by their disguiser, the internal organ, which consists of the three qualities; just as is the case with the redness of such a thing as the [colourless] crystal, produced by the proximity of such a thing as a China rose.

And this mundane condition, just because it is due to a disguiser, is not to be removed by *knowledge*, but by the destruction of (1) the disguiser or (2) the disguised, one or other, or else (3) by the destruction of the connexion between them; for not even by the most skilful looking is there cessation of the erroneous perception of redness in the crystal, so long as there is contact with the disguiser [the China rose near it]. Now in the present case [when we discuss our threefold alternative] the destruction of soul is impossible, because the manifestation of all being depends on its existence; nor, again, can the connexion between the two be destroyed, because that is nothing else than the nature of them both [soul being all-pervading and therefore of course in conjunction with the internal organ as well as everything else]. Consequently by exhaustion the third alternative only is left, viz. that the cessation of the error can only arise from the destruction of the disguiser, and not [as Śankara A'chárya and his followers hold] from the knowledge of soul. And for the destruction of the disguiser another cause [than that suggested by Śankara] is to be sought; and this is devotion to the Lord, which, as being something supramundane, is established by the Veda and authoritative tradition [and not by the ordinary processes of perception and inference].

And so in the Bhagavad Gítá (ch. xiv.) the adorable Kṛishṇa himself declares that faith in himself is the cause of liberation, which is defined as the attainment of divine beatitude through the dissolution of the internal organ, which consists of the three qualities; this he declares, beginning [śl. 6],

"Of these 'Goodness,' by reason of its purity, is illumining and healthful; it binds, O sinless one, [the soul which in itself consists of uncaused bliss and unspecialised knowledge] by association with happiness [not intrinsic but occasioned by motives] and by association with knowledge [such as is not absolute and objectless thought, but is associated with objects]. Know that 'foulness,' consisting of desire, arises from association with a thirst; this, O son of Kuntí, binds the embodied soul by association with action [giving rise to merit and demerit,—obstacles alike to liberation]. But know that 'darkness' is born of ignorance, and is the bewilderer of all the embodied ones; it, O Bhárata, binds by carelessness, inertia and sleep;"[1] and winding up with [śl. 26],

"And whoso worships *me* unwavering, with the devotion of faith, he, having passed beyond these qualities, becomes worthy of existing as Brahman."

[1] The translation of this extract is chiefly borrowed from Ballantyne.

And this does not imply that the knowledge of the soul is useless, for knowledge is an auxiliary to devotion [or faith], by washing away the filth of unbelief; but knowledge cannot abolish the imposition of the property [*i.e.* personality] belonging to the disguiser, the internal organ, which is in direct connexion with the soul [any more than the knowledge that he has jaundice will prevent a man's seeing a white shell as yellow]. Hence this is clearly declared in such passages as that [in the Gítá, ch. xiv. 19],

"When he knows what is beyond the qualities[1] he attains my state,"

and again [iv. 41],

"He who by knowledge has cut away all doubt."

And the soul's mundane condition is not [as the Vedántins say] caused by ignorance, so that its removal could be likewise said to be effectible by knowledge, because there is no proof thereof; and also because in the absence of the proper cause, particles of silver, it is impossible that silver should arise from a shell mistaken for it, [and so too this actual world cannot be produced, as they hold, from ignorance, which they declare to be itself unreal]. And moreover, the text, "how, O gentle youth, could it thus be that Being should be produced from Non-being" (Chhándogya Upan. vi. 2), which establishes the existence of the cause as inferred from the existence of the effect, declares the positive reality of the world; and especially do such texts as that (*Ibid.* iii. 14) "whose will is true," etc., declare the reality of the Supreme Lord's creation. Nor has the venerable Bádaráyaṇa asserted in any Sútra that the world was produced from Ignorance; on the contrary, by rejecting the doctrine of a dream creation, he has asserted the reality of the waking world. Nor was this rejection only employed exoterically as an illustration, for there is no proof for such an assumption.

[1] "*i.e.* what underlies the phenomenal."—Ballantyne.

But the theory [which Vedántins allege] that existence, thought and joy are essential [and constitute soul] is not tenable. Joy, etc., are not directly modifications of soul,[1] —for they are perceived as reflected in soul, just as paleness is, [as when a man says 'I am pale,' *ahaṃ gauraḥ*, where the paleness does not really belong to soul but to body, and is reflected on soul]. It is simplest to suppose that the perception of joy, etc., is through an instrument [*i.e.* the internal organ], because perception is an action [which implies an instrument]; and therefore joy, etc., are instrumentally produced by interpenetration,[2] just as sound is produced by the auricular organ.[3] [Joy, etc., thus interpenetrate the mind as a quality its substance, and are only reflected on soul.] Others [as the followers of the Nyáya] hold that joy, etc., reside by interpenetration in their instrument the mind, because joy, etc., are qualities apprehensible by an uncreated organ [as they hold the mind to be], just as sound is apprehensible by an uncreated organ [because consisting of the uncreated ether]. On either view the illustration drawn from sound will equally hold, because joy on the one hand and sound on the other are equally qualities apprehensible by an intangible organ [mind and the auricular organ being alike intangible]. But the proof of the reality of soul is found in the fact that it reveals all existence [for if there were no seer or knower, nothing could be seen or known]. All this will be made clear in the second portion of the third Chapter.

Therefore, since there is a wish[4] to make a full discussion

[1] "As a waxen cube might be one modification of a piece of wax, and a sphere might be another modification of numerically the same piece of wax, when that same cube has been rolled into a ball."—Ballantyne, *note*.

[2] They exist in the mind by interpenetration (or intimate relation) as qualities or affections, not in the soul by identity as essential constituents. In the comm. on Aph. 99 they are called the modifications of the internal organ.

[3] "The auricular organ is that portion of the indivisible ether walled off within the fleshly ear (as a portion of indivisible space is walled off within the limits of a jar)." —Ballantyne.

[4] The Sanskrit Coll. MS. reads *vidhitsá* for *vivitsá*.

of the nature of Faith (*bhakti*), inasmuch as it is the cause of the attainment of man's highest end, just as there was for the same supposed reason, in the Púrva Mímáṃsá, a wish to make a full discussion of the nature of duty (*dharma*), we have the following propounded as the first aphorism.

Now then there is a wish to know faith. (1).

The word 'now' (*atha*) indicates the *commencement* of the discussion,—it does not [as at the opening of Jaimini's aphorisms] indicate *subsequence.*[1] For there is here no necessary subsequence to any preliminary study of the Veda, since it will be hereafter declared that even men of degraded castes are competent to enter upon the present inquiry. Nor does the word '*now*' imply [as in the Vedánta aphorisms[2]] a *subsequence* to a previous acquirement of tranquillity, etc. [as a necessary preliminary]; because it is simply the desire of liberation which makes any one competent to engage in this inquiry into the nature of Faith. Thus there is the following passage in the Śwetáśwatara Upanishad (vi. 18),

"To Him who at the beginning created Brahmá, and who gave the Vedas to him,—to him the God who reveals the knowledge of himself, do I, desirous of liberation, fly for refuge."

Nor again is the word '*now*' intended to imply a benediction [as in the Yoga aphorisms,[3]] [at the commencement of a new work], for its mere utterance [without any reference to its actual meaning] has this auspicious benedictive power. Therefore its true meaning is that the inquiry into the nature of faith is to be entered upon by him who desires liberation.

[1] Thus the Commentator on Jaimini's first Aphorism explains the *atha* there as "now, *i.e.* after studying the Veda while residing in the family of the teacher."

[2] Thus the Commentator on the first Vedânta aphorism, says, "here the word *now* means 'subsequently to the student's attainment of the four requisites,' *i.e.* a perception of the distinction between the eternal and the transient, a scorn of the transient enjoyments of this world or the next, the possession of tranquillity, self-restraint, etc., and the desire of liberation."

[3] Thus the Commentator on the first Yoga Aphorism says, "the word *now* implies the commencement of a new topic and it also serves as a benediction."

The phrase in the aphorism 'a wish to know' implies 'inquiry.' Although 'faith' which is 'an affection fixed on God' is not something to be effected by works like the 'duty' and consequent 'merit' [which are the great topic of the Púrva Mímáṃsá], nor something to be known like Brahman [whose knowledge is set forth as the great end of the Vedánta]; yet even when faith has been perfected by its proper antecedents, viz. good works, mundane and inferior devotion, etc., it is still liable to be destroyed by the weight of such false objections as 'this is not faith,' 'this does not lead to supreme bliss,' 'this aims not at the highest object,'—as a wife's faith in her husband [by unfounded calumnies]. Hence the word 'then' in the aphorism implies that a thorough discussion is favourable to faith just because it helps to abolish these wrong views. 'Because the abolition of false objections is to be expected from it, therefore is there a wish to know the nature of faith,'—this is the full meaning of the Aphorism. Hence we read [in Prahláda's prayer to Vishṇu in the Vishṇu-puráṇa, I. xx. 16], "In whatever thousands of births I may have to pass, O Lord, through them all may my faith in thee, Achyuta, never be shaken;"[1] this very prayer that his faith may remain unshaken implies that he expects that the inevitable attempts to shake it will be counteracted. And therefore the discussion of faith is only so far fruitful as it is ancillary to faith which itself bears the fruit [in the form of the summum bonum].

But it is objected that faith is no proper subject for discussion, because it cannot enter within the range of the ordinary understanding, as it does not assume any practical form belonging to daily life,—the author therefore propounds its characteristic [or definition] in the following aphorism:

In its highest form it is an affection fixed on God (Íśwara). (2).

In the words 'In its highest form it,' we have the subject;

[1] The reading *achalá* for *achyutá* is clearly wrong,—it destroys the play of words on which the force of the original partly depends.

the rest of the sentence is the predicate. The words 'in its highest form' are added to exclude the lower forms [which will be described hereafter]. The words 'on God' have reference to the proper topic of the present work. 'It,' Faith, is thus generally an affection, the object of which is a being who is to be propitiated (or worshipped);[1] but here in this treatise it is a particular affection of the internal organ having the Supreme Being as its object, and its special character is easily known by examining worldly affection, etc. As it has been said by Prahláda, who possessed this highest faith in Vishṇu (Vishṇu Pur. I. xx. 17),

"May a passion as fixed as that which the unreflecting feel for worldly objects, never depart from my heart ever remembering thee."

In this verse by the word 'passion' (*príti*) an affection is meant, inseparably connected with happiness. Otherwise, if *príti* were taken in its other meaning of 'pleasure,' the locative case of 'object' would be inappropriate, as the idea of object is foreign to that of pleasure [for we can speak of the 'subject' and 'cause' of pleasure, but not properly of its 'object']; and the same objection would hold if *príti* were taken to mean the perception of pleasure, for as that perception would have the pleasure as its object, you could not properly talk of the object of an object. Therefore we have taken as our definition the notion of an affection, together with its proper object. Nor need it be suggested that the meaning of the aphorism is 'a pleasure produced by its object,' for the grammarians lay down no rules for a locative as the case of the producing thing. And again, as the passage before quoted, 'let my faith in thee, Achyuta, never be shaken,' proves that God is the object of faith, the same thing must be meant here by the word *príti*, as the two words (*bhakti* and *príti*) both form one continuous sentence. The distinction

[1] *Árádhyavishayakarágatwam.*

between the two passages is that in the first we have the petition for faith in each successive birth, in the second we have the petition that this faith, under the example of an affection for a worldly object, might be always preserved. And we must anyhow bring in the idea of 'affection,' as without affection you cannot have the pleasure produced by an object. And to the same purport is Patanjali's aphorism (Yoga Sútras ii. 7), "Affection [or 'desire,' *rága*] is what dwells on pleasure." This affection it is which is the essence of faith, as will be seen by its being found accompanying all the characteristic marks which will be mentioned hereafter [see Aphor. 43, 44], and it is also proved to be so by its being the simplest explanation. Faith could not be described as partly consisting of remembrance and partly of celebrating with hymns, etc.; because it would not always be found associated with these;[1] nor again could it consist in the mere knowledge of God, because this might be found even in those who hated him. Nor again can it be defined as the knowing God as an object to be propitiated [or worshipped]; for faith is not always found present in [these outward acts of] praise, homage and other acts of worship; and again we should then have to use the expressions 'he is full of faith,' 'he is full of affection,' even in reference to one who by compulsion or through fear had the idea that God is to be propitiated with praise, etc. If you say that we should define faith as 'the knowledge of God as the proper object of worship, accompanied by affection, etc.,' let us rather say that it is simply an affection (as our Aphorism declares); and so in the Bhagavad Gítá (x. 9),

"Those whose thoughts are on me, whose spirits are fixed on me, admonishing one another and always speaking of me, are contented and glad. To these who are ever devoted to me and serve me with affection, I give that devotion of mind by which they attain to me."

[1] *Ananugamát* might be taken as used similarly to the *anugamát* of Vedánta Sút. i. i. 28, 'because they would not be always found to apply.'

Here we have described the faithful devotedness of those whose thoughts and spirits are fixed on Him, but not of those who merely know Him as the proper object of worship. And hence we read in the Smṛiti[1] that even the [ignorant] milkmaids obtained liberation as the fruit of their faith, because their affection was excited by the sight of Kṛishṇa's lovely form. The preposition *anu* (in *anurakti*) is not a mere affix whose separate meaning is merged in the definition, but it is used here to show that the affection arises after (*anu*) the knowledge of the greatness and other attributes of the Adorable One. "If this were so, should we not have to grant that this faith of ours has also the nature of the affection felt towards a father?" We reply, No, because only the world [and not any particular individual] is identical with the Supreme as being His offspring [cf. the Vedic passage, where the father addresses his son, 'thou art myself under the name of a son']. "Ought we not to add, to make our definition complete, that true faith has for its object the Supreme unmodified by any assumption of inferior form?" But this would not include the case of the milkmaids, etc., who had faith in God as conditioned by an external manifestation. Well then, let faith be an affection having as its object the Soul unconditioned by its disguise, intellect (*buddhi*). Thus faith towards an object conditioned by an external manifestation and faith in the infinite Supreme will be equally included.

From the promise of immortality to him who abides in Him. (3).

'To him who abides'—*i.e.* has faith—'in Him,' *i.e.* God,—immortality is promised as the reward in the Chhándogya Upanishad (ii. 23. 2)—"he who abides[2] in Brahman goes to immortality." Therefore any possible indifference to knowing Him, either on the ground of its having no fruit, or only an inferior fruit, is excluded.

[1] Vishṇu Pur. v. 13.
[2] S'ankara explains *brahmasaṃstha* as *brahmaṇi samyag-avasthitaḥ.*

If you say, it is knowledge,—no, because the knowledge of one who hates Him is not an abiding in Him. (4).

"But does not the term 'abiding in Brahman' (*brahma-saṃsthá*) imply only the knowledge of Brahman, and not faith in him; and so knowledge alone has the fruit of immortality annexed to it?" This objection however has no weight, as the term 'abiding in him' must mean faith and not mere knowledge, from the fact that we never use such a phrase as 'abiding' in reference to one who hates the object, however much knowledge of it he may possess. Thus for instance the ministers, friends, etc., who are devoted to a king, may be fitly described as abiding in him, but not his rival kings. We must here bear in mind the well-known principle that the determination of the Vedic sense of a word is just like that of the secular sense. Hence in the legend of Chirakárika (Mahábh. Śántiparva, 9526), in the lines,

"During that time having reflected on that failure of *saṃsthá* in his wife,
The sage spoke thus distressed, shedding tears in his sorrow,"[1]

the phrase *patní-saṃsthá-vyatikrama* means a failure of devotion in the wife towards her husband; hence the word *saṃsthá* is really a synonym for faith (or devotion, *bhakti*). And so too the same meaning is to be concluded with regard to the aphorism of Bádaráyaṇa (Ved. S. i. 7), "Because Liberation is declared of one who abides in Him" (*tan-nishṭhasya*).

And from its inferiority thereto. (5).

Because knowledge fails before faith, as a means to liberation. The 'and' of the aphorism is intended to show that this

[1] This refers to a curious legend of Gautama's dilatory son, Chirakárika. The sage one day offended with his wife had gone to the forest, leaving an order that his son should kill her in his absence. The son however deliberates so long on the pros and cons of the command that his father has time to grow cool and returns to countermand it.

reason is additional to that given before. Thus it is said in the Gítá (vii. 23),

"They who worship the gods go to the gods, those who are devoted to me go likewise to me,"

and so in other passages. Thus too Kṛishṇa's speech to Prahláda (Vishṇu Pur. I. xx. 20),

"As thy mind filled with faith in me wavers not,
So thou, by my favour, shalt even go to Nirváṇa."

"But is it not said in the Śwetáśwatara Upanishad, 'having known Him, a man goes beyond death,—there is no other path for going thither'? Liberation is thus declared in the Śruti to be the fruit of knowing, and therefore, if the passage of Smṛiti seems to contradict it, it must be interpreted in a different sense from the obvious one." We reply, No, for even here 'its inferiority thereto' is allowed. For the word 'beyond-death' (*atimrityu*) is not conventionally used in the sense of 'liberation,' but rather for that which must be present as the indispensable condition in order that one may pass beyond death; and so it should rather express that faith whereby there is a passage beyond death; [since we take it as one word *ati-mṛityum* rather than as two *ati mṛityum*] in accordance with the well-known grammatical paribháshá on Páṇ. ii. 3. 19, which enjoins that the meaning produced by a case-affix (*káraka*) is of superior force to one produced by assuming a complementary construction.[1] We also see that faith does produce this passing beyond death from such lines as those of the Gítá (xii. 7),

"To those, O prince, whose hearts are fixed on me,
I shall ere long be the deliverer from the sea of the world and death."

There is also a text to the same effect in the Veda (Rig V. vii. 59. 12[2]), "We worship Tryambaka, of grateful fragance,

[1] *i.e.* it is better to take *atimṛityum* as one word governed as an accusative case (káraka) by the verb *eti*, than to take *mṛityum* as governed by the preposition *ati* and therefore forming a complementary part of the sentence, and only in indirect connexion with the verb, cf. Páṇ. ii. 3. 19.

[2] It is also quoted in Taitt. Saṃh. . 8. 6.

the augmenter of prosperity; like the cucumber from its stalk, may I be delivered from death, but not from immortality." Here 'worship' (*yajana*) means 'faith' (*bhakti*), since the *kalpa* so explains it.[1] Nor is it any real objection to our interpretation that the word *bhakti* does not occur in the text of the hymn, because this equally applies to 'liberation' [which is not found directly mentioned in it either]. Consequently we learn from the eternal Veda itself the inferiority of knowledge.

But it may be still asked "why should faith be defined as a form of affection?" To meet this, the author replies,

It is an affection from its being the opposite of hatred and from the Vedic expression 'taste.' (6).

Faith (or devotion) deserves to be called an affection, because it is the opposite of hatred. In secular language the terms 'he hates,' 'he is devoted,' are applied to persons whose dispositions are mutually opposed; and amongst men the opposite of hatred is universally acknowledged to be affection, not knowledge. And so in the Vishṇu Puráṇa (IV. xv. 12), having first described Śiśupála's uninterrupted hatred for Kṛishṇa, the Puráṇa goes on to say, "This divine Vishṇu, if named or called to recollection even with uninterrupted hatred, confers a reward which is hard to be obtained by all gods and demons; how much more will he reward them who possess perfect faith?" So too we read in Atri's Smṛiti, "Remembering Kṛishṇa even with hatred, Śiśupála, the son of Damaghosha, went to heaven; how much more one who is wholly intent upon him?" where we also find faith represented as the proper opposite of hatred. And so too we read in the Gítá (xvi. 18),

"Those detractors who hate me [present] in their own and others' bodies,

[1] Ápastamba's kalpa directs that the priests, as they recite these words, are to toss the baked flour cakes into the air, and to wish aloud to receive them from Bhaga, the deity who presides over good fortune (see Taitt. Saṃh. vol. ii. p. 88). Swapneśwara seems to connect *bhaga* with *bhakti*.

Those fierce haters, the vilest of men in their mortal lives,
I continually throw, wicked as they are, into the wombs of demon mothers.
Born in a demon womb, deluded from birth to birth,
And never finding me, O son of Kuntí, they go thence the lowest road."

And as the opposite of this state of mind, it is right that faith should be described (as in Sút. 2) as an affection whose object is God.

Again, from the passage in the Taittiríya Upanishad (ii. 7), "having obtained the taste, he becomes full of joy," a 'taste' whose object is Brahman is understood to be the cause of liberation which is the manifestation of the joy of Brahman. Now this 'taste' is the same as 'affection,' as is clear from the line in the Gítá (ii. 59),

"Taste itself retires, having seen his supreme indifference to taste;"[1]

where taste means affection for worldly objects. In accordance with this we find the very word *anurága* used for 'faith' in the Vishṇu Puráṇa (IV. iv. 4), where, after describing the ascent to heaven of Ráma, Lakshmaṇa and others, it proceeds to say, "the people also of the city of Kośala who had a fervent affection (*anurágina*ḥ) for those incarnate portions of the supreme Vishṇu,—having their minds fixed thereon, obtained possession of the same world with them." Therefore we conclude that not knowledge, but 'faith' in the form of affection has supreme bliss as its fruit.

"But is it not wrong to take opposition to hatred as the characteristic mark of affection, because this will equally apply

[1] I have followed Schlegel in his translation of this line, as the author of the Commentary seems to have explained it in some such way, or he would have hardly quoted it alone without the preceding line. The Commentators on the Bhagavad Gítá all take *rasavarjam* as for *rasam varjayitwá*. "In the case of the embodied soul which forbears to grasp (as in fasting), the different external objects retire, leaving only desire behind; but desire itself retires, when it beholds the Supreme Soul in him (the wise man)."

to indifference and thus include too much?" We reply that the proper effect of hatred is a cessation [from all acts of kindness, etc.], and the true opposite of this frame of mind must be a state of action [which would not apply to indifference]; and we see this action in the earnest following of the devoted after the object of their devotion, while in the case of those who have the opposite feeling we find an entire cessation from this following. Hence the phrase 'the opposite of hatred' is used in the Aphorism, with an eye to this opposition between them as manifested by their respective effects. The argument (when drawn out in the full technical form[1]) will be as follows: Faith must be an affection directed to a particular object—from the fact of its being a particular quality of the soul, which is different from any merely selfish feeling as to that object being the means of attaining one's own interest, and which yet produces as its effect a following of the object, etc.; whatever is not so, is not so [*i.e.* whatever is not an affection will not have the two subjoined characteristics], as, for instance, hatred. And another ground of our definition is found in the fact that we see with the increase of the affection a correspondent increase in the following of the object, etc.[2] And again, we may put it in this form; whoever is devoted to a certain object, (the absence of indifference being clearly understood) in him resides that particular quality which we call 'faith' [or 'devotion,']—a quality which must be the opposite of hatred and tend to produce a following of the object, from the fact that it is a special quality of the soul producing this following; just as is seen in the parallel case where there is the feeling that such and such an object will be a means of obtaining one's own interest.[3] Thus we conclude that it is an affection, and at the same time show that

[1] For this form of the syllogism, see my note, Colebrooke's Essays, vol. i. p. 315. What follows is only to repeat ll. 1–10 in a technical form.

[2] This is interesting as an instance of Mill's Method of Concomitant Variations.

[3] This feeling is also the opposite of hatred and tends to produce a following of the object from the same reason.

it is different from the feeling of promoting one's own interest [as this latter feeling can be itself used as an illustration of the working of faith, and therefore of course cannot be identical with it]. And again, the argument *à fortiori* 'how much more so, in the case of the devoted?' only holds good with regard to a quality opposite to hatred, as in the Gítá (ix. 32), "They who fly to me for refuge, even though born in mean births, [obtain salvation;] how much more then holy Bráhmans and pious royal sages?" So by that previously-quoted passage in the Gítá (xvi. 18), where Kṛishṇa says that he throws into demon births those who hate him, he shows that as hatred is the cause of transmigration and worldly existence, so its opposite, an affection directed towards the Supreme Being, in the form of 'faith,' causes the abolition of all worldly existence by destroying [the internal organ which is] the disguise of the soul. This is expressly declared in that line,

"Never finding me, O son of Kuntí, they go thence the lowest road."

From the expression 'and' in the Aphorism we infer that faith is also an affection, because it possesses the characteristic signs of earthly affection, such as horripilation, etc. Thus there is a well-known passage in the Śakuntalá (Act iii.[1]), where the king says,

"She reveals her affection for me by her cheek with its down erect."

But if faith were a different quality of the soul, there would be a needless complication in having to assume a special set of characteristic signs for it [which in themselves were not new].

Some authors hold that Affection is a species of 'wish' as it also arises from the knowledge of the fact that its object will produce a desired end, as is the case in sacrifice, etc. But we hold that 'affection' is distinct from 'wish,' just as hatred is, and this we infer from the facts of consciousness, as we can

[1] This is quoted from the Bengali recension.

feel, 'I love, I have an affection for, and yet I do not wish for,'—since 'wish' refers only to what one has not attained, but affection refers equally to what is attained and what is not; and indeed it would only be a useless complication, to endeavour to show that it is always to be defined as a wish. This is a summary of what can be said on the subject; and we therefore consider that our definition has been now established to be correct.

"But is not faith an action? and an action is not competent to produce supreme bliss, according to such passages in Śruti as that [in the Taittiríya Ároṇyaka, x. 10. 21] 'not by work, nor offspring, nor wealth, but by abandonment of all these have some attained to immortality.'"

The author proceeds to refute this doubt in the next aphorism.

It is not an action, for, like knowledge, it does not depend on effort. (7).

This faith cannot properly be an action, because it does not follow an effort of will.[1] Whatever does not follow an effort of will, is not an action, as for instance knowledge; for knowledge depends on the presence of the proper evidence, and a man cannot, at his pleasure, produce it or not, or alter it. And so too with faith. The affection felt by its subject towards a beautiful woman, children, etc., cannot be produced in its different manifestations by the man's own exertions alone; but in the case of the devotion which we speak of, it depends on the man's good deeds in former births, inferior devotion,[2] etc.

Hence indeed is the endlessness of its fruit. (8).

Since faith is not an action, its fruit, beatitude, is rightly

[1] There is an important technical śloka current among the Paṇḍits, *Jnána-janyá bhaved ichchhá, ichchhá-janyá bhavet kṛitiḥ, kṛiti-janyá bhavech-cheshṭá, cheshṭá-janyá bhavet kriyá. Kṛiti* here means *yatna* 'volition.' "From knowledge arises desire (βούλησις), from desire volition (προαίρεσις), from volition conscious exertion of the muscles (ὄρεξις), and from this action."

[2] For this, see infra, Aph. 56, etc.

held to be endless. If it were an action, even immortality [which the Chhándogya Upanishad promises as its reward, see Aph. 3] would have to come to an end, in accordance with that text of the same Upanishad (viii. 1. 6), "Just as here the world gained by work perishes, so too hereafter the world gained by merit perishes."

And from the use of the word 'worship' (prapatti) in the case of one who has knowledge, faith is not knowledge, as in other cases where 'worship' is used. (9).

Kṛishṇa says in the Gítá (vii. 19),

"After many births he who has knowledge worships me;
One who knows that Vásudeva is all,—such a great-souled one is hard to be found."

This 'worship'[1] is spoken of as pertaining to one who has knowledge; and this would be unsuitable, if faith were the cause of knowledge [and not rather, as we hold, its consequence]; as we see also in other cases where the same word 'worship' is similarly used. Thus immediately after the passage just quoted from the Gítá, we read

"Having their knowledge carried away by various desires, they worship other deities."

By this passage, which is meant to blame the worship of other deities, the worship of the Supreme is indirectly praised.[2] By this word 'worship' faith towards the deities is really meant and not the knowledge of them; for this is the only sense of the word which we can recognize as used in both cases. From the use of the word 'and' in the Aphorism, we infer that the mention, in the Gítá, of faith [implied in 'worship'] as subsequent to knowledge, is another reason for faith not being the same as knowledge. Thus we read in the Gítá (xv. 19),

[1] The Comm. on Bh. G. explains *prapadyate* here as *bhajati*; *prapatti* therefore = *bhakti*, *i.e.* devoted worship.

[2] The MS. in the Calcutta Sanskrit Coll. Library reads ईश्वरप्रपत्तिः for प्रपत्तिः.

"Whosoever unconfounded knows me Purushottama,
He knowing all, O Bhárata, worships me as identical with all things."[1]

And so too again (ix. 13),

"Having known me the first of beings and indestructible, they worship me with minds entirely fixed on me,"

and again (x. 8),

"Thus having known, the wise worship me, filled with rapture."

Therefore faith is not the same as knowledge.

Although, from the very fact of its being an affection, it is certain that it is different from knowledge, this discussion is needed to obviate a doubt which might otherwise arise, that the word 'faith' might mean, in a secondary sense, the knowledge of Brahman.

Here, however, a question is raised,—"the words of the Bhagavad-Gítá are not a direct authority in the form of 'inspired words' (*śabda*) as the Vedas are, but only secondarily as 'tradition' (*smṛiti*), as being comprised in the Bhárata, and hence how can the Aphorism lay such stress on the 'word'?" Here some explain it as meaning the inferred word [*i.e.* it is inferred that what is in an inspired book of tradition like the Gítá must be found somewhere in the Veda, all Smṛiti deriving from thence its authority]. We however affirm that what constitutes a Veda is the fact of its being uttered by a divine Person and relating to an unseen object, and this character is not wanting in the Gítá. Hence we see the well-known epigraph at the end of each section "*Iti bhagavad-gításúpanishatsu*;" and these ślokas have been only recorded[2] [not composed] by Vyása. And thus declares another Puráṇa,

[1] So S'ankara; S'rídharaswámin explains *sarvabhávena* as 'in every way' (*sarvaprakáreṇa*).

[2] Cf. Manu, viii. 255, "What the witnesses, thus assembled and interrogated, shall positively declare concerning the limits, let him record (*nibadhníyát*) in writing, together with all their names."

"The Gítá is to be attentively recited,—what need is there of other long compilations of śástras?
That Gítá, which itself issued from the lotus-mouth of Padmanábha."

Nor is there any fear of its thus coming within the prohibition which forbids a śúdra to hear [as is the case with regard to the Veda],—because that is certainly settled by the general permission for all castes to hear the Bhárata,[1] just as is allowed to be the case with passages praising Om, etc. If our opponent should maintain that the Bhárata is meant for all castes, excluding the Gítá, we reply that without the Gítá the well-known sum-total of 100,000 ślokas could not be completed. And thus has it been declared by the teachers, "Those mantras of the Vedas, inserted in the Bhárata, etc., they use in a secular sense, omitting the rules of their private reading."

Thus ends the first daily portion of the first chapter of the Commentary on the hundred Aphorisms of Śáṇḍilya composed by the most learned teacher Swapneśwara.

Faith having been defined as a direct cause of immortality, the second daily portion is here commenced to discuss the nature of knowledge, concentration, and faith, as respectively the means and the end.

This [faith] is the main thing, since the others depend upon it. (10).

The word 'this' is used in the Aphorism to remind the reader of what was mentioned at the close of the first daily portion. This highest form of faith is the main or principal thing, since it is regarded by the others, the knowledge of soul, concentration, etc., as the end to which they are to be subordinated. Thus in the Chhándogya Upanishad, after the passage begin-

[1] Cf. the current lines, "The three Vedas are not to be heard by women, śúdras, or titular Bráhmans; so the sage through pity composed the Bhárata narrative."

ning "that which is immensity is felicity," we read (vii. 24), "the soul is all this; seeing thus, thinking thus, knowing thus, he becomes devoted to the soul, rejoicing in the soul, mated to the soul, having his happiness in the soul, he becomes self-resplendent." Here the idea of 'sight,' as implied in the words 'seeing thus,' is used as subsidiary to the highest faith, described by the words 'devoted to the soul' (*átma-ratiḥ*), with a view to remove the error that it is not lovable, etc. As in such cases as 'the ascetic [or 'staff-bearer'] repeats the initiatory phrase after his guru,' 'he causes the cow to be milked, himself wearing his thread reversed,' 'knowing he offers,' 'being wealthy he is happy,' etc., the words 'staff,' etc., are subsidiary,—so here too 'seeing' is subsidiary to faith; and the other things, 'thinking' and 'knowing,' are added over and above as not irrelevant, inasmuch as they are conducive to what is mentioned as the main point. So too 'rejoicing in the soul,' etc., are a relevant repetition, inasmuch as rejoicing is always found present where devotedness is; otherwise the clauses of the sentence quoted would be divided, and 'devotedness' would be the subject, and 'seeing,' etc., would be the predicate, or *vice versâ* [*i.e.* the clauses would not be consecutive attributes of one and the same subject]. Therefore the 'seeing' is subsidiary, according to the rule of the Prior Mímáṃsá (iii. 1. 2), "it is subsidiary because it subserves another thing as its end." Hence the divine sage[1] (Mahábh. Śánti P. ch. 194) declares the superior excellence of one devoted to the soul,

"He who abandoning his natural actions, in deep meditation, is always devoted to the soul,
Becoming himself the soul of all beings, goes thereby the highest road."[2]

[1] *i.e.* Bhíshma. The Bibl. Indica text reads *Manu*, but the Sanskrit Coll. MS. reads *muniḥ* for *manuḥ*.

[2] I follow here the Mahábhárata text *sarvabhútátmabhús tasmát sa gachchhed uttamáṃ gatim.*

And from the subject-matter's belonging to faith. (11).

Faith [as described by 'devotedness'] constitutes the subject-matter from its having the end bound up with it; therefore 'seeing,' as being included as a means thereto, can only be subsidiary.

If you say 'it is the effect of seeing,'—no, because the pronoun 'tad' is interposed. (12).

"But may we not say, 'Immortality defined as self-resplendency, is really the effect of seeing, and so it is just the reverse of what you have been maintaining,—*i.e.* seeing will be the subject-matter?'" we reply, No, because the pronoun *tad* is interposed, "*he* becomes self-resplendent." By this word 'he,' the subject close at hand is represented, *i.e.* 'the one devoted to soul,' and not the more remote subject 'seeing,' since there is no reason why that which is separated should be brought into close contiguity. If you maintain that its being the subject-matter is itself a sufficient reason [why 'seeing' should be meant], we reply that this would be a case of the logical fault of 'mutual dependence' (*i.e.* reasoning in a circle).

And from visible experience. (13).

We see in common life that the knowledge of his beauty causes affection for a young man in a girl's mind,[1] but affection does not cause knowledge. Hence we conclude that knowledge is a subsidiary, because we see by experience that it aids affection. And again we see that the knowledge that 'nature' is pitiless, limited, unlovely, etc., causes distress of mind to living beings, while the knowledge that Soul is all-merciful, of unlimited power and infinite beauty, dispels distress; and hence arises the highest form of faith.

Hence it is said in the Gítá (v. 17),

"They who think of the Supreme, whose souls are bound up in Him, who abide in Him, and find their refuge in Him,

[1] Cf. Damayantí's love for Nala.

They go thither whence there is no return, having all their sins removed by knowledge."

And so too in the A'yurveda,[1]

"Thought, firmness, and knowledge of soul, etc., are the best medicine of the mind's ailings."

And therefore from the absence of knowledge in the case of the milkmaids. (14).

Since knowledge is thus a means, as being manifestly subservient, the Smṛiti, rejecting all visible means, declares that the milkmaids attained liberation solely by devotion to the Supreme One, from the consequent abolition of all foulness of mind, etc. As we read in the Vishṇu Puráṇa (V. xiii. 13),

"One virtuous damsel, having all her merits cancelled by the intense rapture of thinking about Him, and all her sins expiated by the agony of not obtaining Him,—meditating on Him, the cause of the world, identical with the supreme Brahman,—ceasing to breathe, obtained liberation."

Here the presence of deep devotion is inferred by its signs of pleasure and pain, and thereby[2] liberation; such is the meaning of the passage. Just as you can obtain the fruit of the sacrifice with unshelled golden berries and thus obviate all need for any intermediate operation,[3] so in the case of the milkmaids we have liberation produced directly by affection; and hence knowledge is clearly understood to be only a subsidiary means; but if knowledge were the main end, no fruit would be produced in its absence. Nor can you say that the

[1] This occurs in the Ashṭánga-hṛidaya, i. 23; for an account of this medical treatise by Vágbhaṭa, see Prof. Weber's Catal. Berlin Libr. No. 929–934.

[2] The Bibl. Ind. has a bad misreading *na* for *tena* in p. 15, l. 6 infra; the Sanskrit Coll. MS. has *tena*.

[3] *i.e.* knowledge produces the removal of *málinya* and that causes *bhakti* and that liberation; but if there be no *málinya* there is no need of *jnána*, but you can have *bhakti* at once and then *mukti*, as the unlearned *gopís* had; just as in making an oblation of boiled rice you must first shell the rice; but if you make an offering of golden grains (an offering described in the Nyáya-málá-vistara, x. i. 1), you have the result at once without the trouble of shelling. *Avaghúta*=*jnána*, and the husk= *málinya*.

milkmaid's intense thinking about Him could be the required knowledge of the identity of the soul and Brahman,—because there could not be the recognised concurrent causes of knowledge, as hearing, pondering, etc.; but it is merely a case of remembrance closely bound up with affection. Nor is it to be explained as a case of 'persuasive enforcement of a previous injunction' [i.e. *arthaváda*,—'knowledge' being really intended, and 'affection' being only brought in to illustrate it—], because the subject had not been mentioned before [so there could be no such enforcement]; and there is no direct 'injunction' near [as there should be to constitute a true *arthaváda*].

If you say 'he knows by his faith,' we reply 'no,' because it is 'repeated knowledge' which is thus aided by faith. (15).

The opponent now urges the fact that this view directly contradicts *śruti* and consequently all arguments based on the 'subject-matter' (Aph. 11), 'relative position' (Aph. 12), and 'sign' (Aph. 14) are precluded.[1]—"Thus it is expressly declared in the Gítá (xviii. 55),

[1] The Mímâṃsâ arranges the proofs that one thing is ancillary to another, in the following order. 1. *S'ruti* or a definite text, as 'let him offer with curds,' where curds are clearly an ancillary part of the sacrifice. 2. *Liṅga* 'sign' or 'the sense of the words,' as leading to an inference, as in the text 'he divides by the ladle;' here we infer that the thing divided must be a liquid like ghee, since a ladle could not divide solid things like the baked flour cakes. 3. *Vákya* 'the being mentioned in one sentence;' as in the text "'(I cut) thee for food' thus saying, he cuts the branch;" here the words '(I cut) thee for food' are ancillary to the action of cutting. 4. *Prakaraṇa* 'the subject-matter viewed as a whole with an interdependence of its parts,' as in the *darśa-púrṇamása* sacrifice, where the *prayája* ceremonies, which have no special fruit mentioned, produce, as parts, a mystic influence (*apúrva*) which helps forward that influence of the whole by which the worshippers obtain heaven. Here the *prakaraṇa* proves them to be ancillary. 5. *Sthána* 'relative position' or 'order,' as the recital of the hymn *śundadhwam*, etc., 'be ye purified for the divine work' in connexion with the mention of the *sánnáyya* vessels, where this position proves that the hymn is ancillary to the action of sprinkling those vessels. 6. *Samákhyá* 'title,' thus the Yajurveda is called the special book for the adhwaryu priests, hence in any rite mentioned in it they are primâ facie to be considered as the priests employed. The order represents the relative weight attached to each, the first, *śruti*, being the most important, the last, *samákhyá*, the least. (Cf. Jaimini's *Sútras*, iii. 3. 1-14; *Nyáyamáláviat.*, iii. 3. 1-11; *Mímâṃsáparibhâshá*, pp. 8, 9; *Vedánta-sútras*, iii. 3. 44, 49). The objector in the text maintains that (4) (5) and (2) are precluded here by the *śruti* (1) from the Bhagavad-gítá.

'By faith he really recognises me, how great and what I am;
Then having really known me, he forthwith enters into me.'

Now just as in the sentence (Taitt. Śaṃh. i. 5. 8) 'he draws near to the gárhapatya fire with an Aindrí verse,' [the word *aindryá* implies the instrument,] so here, according to the rule mentioned above that 'the meaning produced by a case-affix is of superior force' in Śruti as well as in secular writings, it follows that faith (being in the instrumental case) is to be considered as the cause of knowledge. With regard to the Aphorism 'from visible experience' (Aph. 13), although there is no need to refer to Śruti, where we have the aid of visible experience and the matter is within the range of sense-perception, perception fails to inform us how far an affection towards Brahman is to be aided by knowledge. The fact that we see knowledge have such an effect in the case of the love of a young girl, etc., is, I allow, a primâ facie ground for a similar inference in regard to the affection towards Brahman; but all that this reasoning could end in would be a 'sign,' leading to an inference, [but, as we have said, this is precluded, as we have a direct text of the Gítá in opposition to it]."

We reply, if the Gítá had used the words "he cognises me" only (*jánáti*), we should have granted what you say; but its term is *abhijánáti*, and this implies the knowledge of something already previously known. So the first knowledge is ancillary to faith and promotes faith as its fruit; afterwards faith seeks to aid knowledge when strengthened by repetition in the form of *abhijná* or 'revised knowledge,' just as we have the shelling of the rice by repeated acts of shelling separate grains. The latter part of the verse is added to correct the impression which might be produced by this aid rendered by the effect 'faith' [to its cause 'knowledge'],—"then," *i.e.* after faith has been strengthened by the strengthening of knowledge, "he enters." Therefore this is not properly to be called a *śruti*, but rather a confirmatory repetition (*anuváda*) obtained by a deduction of reason.

He explains this still further.

And this had been declared before. (16).

Before the lines in the Gítá (xviii. 55) "by faith he recognises me,"—after having declared "he becomes fitted for union with Brahman," Kṛishṇa goes on to say (xviii. 54),

"Having become Brahman, being contented in soul, he grieves not, nor desires,
Feeling perfect equanimity towards all beings, he obtains the highest faith in me."

Since the devotee, as one who knows Brahman [by being united to Him][1] has no need for further knowledge, we can only take the following lines as an illustrative repetition [and not a fresh declaration of Śruti].

Therefore even an alternative view is rejected. (17).

By our thus settling the position of knowledge as a means, any attempt to consider knowledge and faith as possibly alternative ends, is precluded. There can be no alternative with regard to an end and a means. The word 'even' in the aphorism implies that still more is the view of their both being held as ends together, precluded.

'Faith towards a god' applies to something other than the supreme, because it is coupled with something else. (18).

It is said by the Śruti somewhere (Śwetáśw. Up. vi. 23),

"He who has supreme faith towards a god, and as towards a god, so towards a teacher,
To him verily great of soul all these objects as declared reveal themselves."

Here the expression 'faith towards a god' must be understood as relating to a being other than the Supreme Íśwara, because it is coupled with faith towards the teacher, for there can be no such juxtaposition in the case of that highest form

[1] In p. 17, l. 3, read ज्ञातब्रह्मणो with Ballantyne's MS. (Ind. Office Lib.) and Sansk. Coll. MS.

of faith, which leads as its fruit to immortality. But we do not dispute that Indra and the other gods, when worshipped, promote the fruit, knowledge, as they do good fortune.[1] This is what the close connexion proves, just as the meaning of the word *ulúka* is proved by the connexion [of the context, *i.e.* whether it means in a given place Kaṇáda or an owl[2]]. This explanation is added as confirmatory of the previous argument.

But concentration is for both, since it looks both ways like the prayája. (19).

Concentration on the other hand is subsidiary to knowledge and to faith, since fixedness of mind is necessary to both. "But may we not apply here the principle of the *Púrva Mímáṃsá* (iii. 1. 22) that 'subsidiary portions of a sacrifice stand as such on the same level and so cannot be connected with each other;' and therefore how can concentration, which is subsidiary to the principal end (faith), be also subsidiary to the means (knowledge)?"

He replies "like the *prayája*." As the *prayája* ceremony is subsidiary to the *vájapeya* sacrifice, and is also subsidiary to the *díkshaṇíyá* which is a part thereof, so it is here, since there is the same proof to establish *yoga* as being subsidiary to both. Or we may perhaps say that concentration, which was originally undertaken as subsidiary only to knowledge,[3] is accidentally [or secondarily] conducive to faith. In the same way we must consider that indifference to worldly objects is conducive to both.

"But is it not hard to go counter to the traditional teaching of Patanjali [in the Yoga-sútras, i. 23], in the aphorism, 'from the meditation on God,' where the worship of the Supreme, as implied by the word 'meditation,' is meant to be conducive to

[1] The Sansk. Coll. MS. reads *śruta-phalavat* for *śubhavat*, a var. lect. which serves as a comment.

[2] This explanation of *ulúkavat* is merely conjectural.

[3] In p. 18, l. 5, I read with Sans. Coll. MS. योगानुष्ठानं.

the attainment of mystic contemplation; and so how can faith be the principal thing?" He replies,

It is by the lower form of faith that mystic contemplation is produced. (20).

The 'meditation' here mentioned is the lower, not the higher, form of faith; and by *it* is mystic contemplation produced,—hence there is no contradiction whatever with the doctrine of Patanjali. And to the same purport are the two succeeding aphorisms of the *Yoga,* "His name is Om," "Its repetition and reflection on its meaning."

If you say 'faith is to be avoided as being an affection,'—no, because it has the highest aim, like union. (21).

This aphorism is introduced incidentally from the mention of the Yoga-śástra. It may be said that faith also should be altogether avoided by one who wishes for liberation, because it does not differ from the affection characterized [and condemned] in the Yoga Aphorisms (ii. 3), "affection, aversion, and tenacity of mundane existence are the 'afflictions.'" But this is not a true view, because faith has the highest aim, as its object is I'śwara. A certain feeling is not to be avoided from the mere fact of its being an affection, but from its being an affection connected with mundane existence; just in the same way as it is not mere 'union' that is to be avoided but union with what is evil, [for to be in a state of union with God is a state devoutly to be desired]. And so in this alleged inference, "faith in I'śwara is to be avoided, because it is an affection," we must supply the limiting condition (or upádhi) which is required to narrow its too great comprehensiveness, viz. its being connected with mundane existence or its not being conducive to liberation. And this faith is not devoid of the quality of 'goodness,' for this is expressly declared to be its characteristic, in that line of the Gítá (xvii. 4) "those with the quality of goodness worship the gods," etc.

This [faith] indeed [is the highest] from the express declaration of its superiority to the performers of sacrificial acts, to those who follow knowledge, and to those who practise concentration. (22).

This form of worship is indeed the highest,—this faith has the highest character. This is every way ascertained, since the Gítá declares (vi. 46, 47),

"The yogí is higher than the ascetics, he is counted higher than even those who follow knowledge,
The yogí is higher than those who perform sacrificial acts; therefore, O Arjuna, be thou a yogí.
And of all yogís, whosoever with his soul intent on me
In full belief worships me, he is accounted by me the most devoted."

Here there is to be understood a gradual climax of the different subjects, caused by the successive superiority of their respective characteristics, asceticism, etc.; but of course no subsidiary can be reckoned superior to its end; therefore faith is the principal.

The author now quotes a passage to avoid the possibility of this erroneous tenet rising up as if it were countenanced by the supposed purport of śruti [as had been attempted by the objector, in § 15].

From the question of the superiority of faith having been settled by question and answer. (23).

Here the whole of the twelfth chapter of the Gítá is an example in point. Arjuna's opening words form the question;

"They who in faith worship thee, thus constantly devoted to thee,
And they who worship the indestructible and the unmanifested,—which of these knows most of *yoga*?"

The answer follows,

"They who fixing their mind on me, worship me, ever devoted,

Endowed with the highest belief, they are counted by me the most devoted.[1]

But they[2] who worship the indestructible, the indescribable, and the unmanifested,

The all-pervading, the inconceivable, the unchangeable, the unmoved, the permanent,

Restraining all their senses, indifferently affected towards all,

These verily attain me, being intent on the welfare of all.

Their labour is the greater who fix their thoughts on the unmanifested,

The path of the unmanifested is with difficulty obtained by embodied beings.

But they who are intent on me, having transferred all their actions to me,

And worship me, contemplating me with unfaltering concentration,

To them a deliverer from the sea of death and the world

I shall ere long be, son of Pṛithá, as their thoughts are fixed upon me."

As this question and answer definitely determine the superiority of faith to knowledge, this passage cannot be considered as only a rhetorical description [i.e. *arthaváda,* but it is to be accepted as an authoritative statement]. In other words the dialogue is intended to settle a doubt, not to commend faith. The point insisted on is, that to pursue the subsidiary path [of knowledge, apart from faith,] only leads to additional toil.

The mention of belief (*śraddhá* in the extract from the Gítá, śl. 2) brings in a doubt that faith (*bhakti*) may be a kind of belief (*śraddhá*); he proceeds to lay this demon.

But it is not the same as belief, because it has a wider range. (24).

Faith must not be universally supposed to be identical with

[1] These have faith (*bhakti*).

[2] These have knowledge, and according to S'áṇḍilya's view follow the lower and more rugged path.

belief (*śraddhá*), because belief is merely subsidiary to ceremonial works; but not so is faith in Íśwara.

And because there would be a regressus ad infinitum, if faith were the same as that [i.e. belief.] (25).

It is said in the Śruti (Gítá, vi. 47),

"He who, believing, has faith in me, is accounted by me the most devoted."[1]

[Now faith cannot be the same as belief for three reasons.]

i. For if faith were really the same as belief, this verse which declares belief to be a subsidiary part of faith would involve an *ad infinitum regressus*, and therefore belief cannot be thus subsidiary to itself. For under your view we should have one belief a subsidiary part of another belief, since you hold that faith is only the same as belief; and as this same subsidiary belief would be itself faith, you would next have to assume a new belief to be in turn *its* subsidiary part, and this in the same way would require a third, and so on ad infinitum.

ii. Again, just as the opening verses of a ceremony[2] do not require any opening verses to be subsidiary to themselves; and the rinsing the mouth (which is a preliminary to all ceremonial acts) does not require a preliminary rinsing for itself [as each would thus involve a similar *regressus ad infinitum*]; so [if faith were really the same as belief] it would not require a preliminary belief as its subsidiary part; [but this is definitely settled by the verse from the Gítá; and consequently our assumption of the identity of faith and belief which led to this contradiction of Śruti, must be false].

iii. And a third argument against the identity in question is found in the ordinary phrase 'endowed with belief and faith,' which directly speaks of them as distinct.

[1] Here 'belief' is subsidiary to 'faith,' according to the rule 'that which characterizes the agent is a subsidiary part of the ceremony to be performed;' as in the injunction "let him who desires heaven offer the sacrifice," where the desire of heaven is considered to be subsidiary.

[2] For the *árambhaṇíyáḥ*, cf. Ait. Bráhm. vi. 6.

But the Brahma-káṇḍa is directed to faith as its end, since with regard to its producing subsequent 'knowledge' it is only on a level [with the púrva-káṇḍa]. (26).

He now replies to the objector who says, that, "if knowledge were not the principal end, the *uttara-káṇḍa* or latter part of the Veda [*i.e.* the Upanishads] would not have been universally considered to be the portion which treats of knowledge [as opposed to the *púrva* or *karma-káṇḍa,* which treats of ceremonial works]." The portion of the Veda which treats of Brahman is revealed for the sake of faith, not for the sake of knowledge, since the object of both káṇḍas is equally to declare what was previously unknown; otherwise, we should have had a *jnána-káṇḍa,* declaring the knowledge of ceremonial duty, revealed in the *púrvakáṇḍa.* Nor is there any positive injunction (*vidhi*) in regard to knowledge, which, by its own predominant force as *vidhi,* might thus lend an authority to the *jnána-káṇḍa* as such. Therefore the general idea of the *jnána-káṇḍa* is a mistake; it should be properly called the *brahma-káṇḍa.* Hence we find it expressly said in the Brahma-sútras, "Now, then, there is a desire to know Brahman."[1] It is therefore also a *bhaktikáṇḍa,* as its true end is faith.

Thus ends the second daily portion of the first chapter of the Commentary on the hundred Aphorisms of Śáṇḍilya, composed by the most learned teacher Swapneśwara.

---

[1] *i.e.* it is *brahma-jijnásá* and not *jnána-jijnásá*; it should be therefore *bhakti-káṇḍa,* not *jnána-káṇḍa.*

SECOND CHAPTER.

As this faith is not directly to be produced by effort, other means for its attainment are to be looked for; of these means the one most closely connected is knowledge, the extraneous ones are inferior faith, etc.; the author therefore here commences this second chapter to ascertain what these respective means are.

The practice of the means of knowledge is to be continued until purification is produced, as in shelling rice. (27).

'Knowledge' is the certain knowledge concerning Brahman. Although this is not to be attained by mere effort, still the practice of the means thereto, such as hearing, considering, profound meditation, etc., is indispensable for its attainment. "But are we to understand that the student is to practise once for all, according to the rule that 'the meaning of the śástra is fulfilled when once performed,' or is he to continue to practise it until his faith is thoroughly confirmed?" To this it is thus replied. It is necessary to practise hearing and the rest until faith is completely purified; just as in the rule "he shells the rice," the meaning of the śástra is that the man is to continue the pounding until the rice is completely cleared of its husk, so from the analogy of this visible example the student must strive to practise knowledge and the other means until he has abolished the mind's foulness.

If it be [ironically] suggested that it does not follow that the means subordinate to these means should themselves be practised,—the next aphorism supplies the answer.

And of their respective means. (28).

It is also proper to practise the respective means which are themselves subordinate to those direct means of producing knowledge, *i.e.* such subordinate means as following the teacher, studying such doctrines as are not contradictory to the Veda, tranquillity, etc. The primary means are not able to produce the end without their subordinate means, just as the general is useless without his army.

The question is next discussed as to the purification of the objects of the understanding.

Káśyapa holds that the understanding should be fixed on omnipotence, from its being other. (29).

The teacher Káśyapa[1] holds that the understanding obtains supreme bliss as its end when it has as its object a Being endowed with the Supreme I'śwara's attributes, as omnipotence, etc. Why so? because this Supreme Being is 'other' than all individual souls, and those individual souls depend on the knowledge of this 'other' in order to know themselves. In this theory there is an absolute difference between the individual soul and Brahman.

Bádaráyaṇa holds that it should be fixed on Soul alone. (30).

The teacher Bádaráyaṇa on the other hand holds that it should have as its object pure Soul, and so the Brahma-sútra (iv. 1. 3), "but they recognise and declare it as the Soul." In this doctrine, as the notion that the individual soul is Brahman is really false [as there is properly no such thing as an individual soul at all], and the only positive truth is the knowledge of the one soul as essential intelligence, this alone leads to liberation.

Śáṇḍilya holds that it should be fixed on both, [inferring it] from the revealed word and reason. (31).

The teacher Śáṇḍilya, however, holds that it should be fixed on both,—why? because 'the revealed word,' the Veda, declares so (Chhánd. Up. iii. 14). After beginning, "All

[1] I do not know who this teacher is,—his doctrine evidently corresponds to that of Rámánuja.

this verily is Brahman, for thence doth it proceed, therein doth it merge and therein doth it live, thus let him worship it with a tranquil mind," it then goes on, "this is my soul within my heart, this is Brahman, this shall I obtain, having passed from hence. He who is sure of this and has no doubt, [becomes Brahman]; thus saith the teacher Śáṇḍilya." Thus having discussed the point, the Veda declares that he who knows both objects, obtains the end of becoming Brahman, which is produced by faith and love, defined as directed to Brahman. There is no real contradiction [as a thoroughgoing Mímáṃsist, who holds the eternity of the Veda, might object] in consequence of a juxtaposition of the eternal and the non-eternal in the same sacred text, because it is to be explained as referring to some former Śáṇḍilya, just as in the similar mention of an individual name in the well-known passage, "Babara Práváhaṇi desired" (Taitt. Saṃh. vii. 1. 10).[1] But in reality the Veda is to be regarded as having the Supreme as its author, [but not as having existed from all eternity.] And the same thing is to be inferred from the text,[2] "from that universal sacrifice sprang the Ṛich and Sáman verses, the metres sprang from it, from it the yajus arose."

The same view can also be established by reason. Brahman is described in the Veda as possessing all power and also as being identical with the individual soul. Thus the Śruti says (Taittiríya Upan. iii. 1), "From whom verily these beings are born, by whom, when born, they live, whom they approach, whom they enter,—him do thou seek to know." And so in the Gítá (xv. 7),

> "A portion of me is in the animate world, become the individual soul, eternal."

In these circumstances what can destroy what? Therefore such sentences as that in the Chhándogya 'that art thou,' etc., prove that both should be known.

1 Cf. Muir's *Sanskrit Texts*, vol. iii. p. 77, etc.
2 Ṛig V. x. 90. Taittiríya A'raṇyaka, iii. 12. 4.

If you say this is impossible from the incompatibility,—not so,—because each may want certain special characteristics [without affecting the partial identity] as in the case of two recognitions. (32).

"But is not the view that this knowledge is to have both as its objects, impossible from the incompatibility of the two objects? for the knowledge of an object distinguished by its inability to create the world, etc., is incompatible with an object distinguished by this very creative power, etc." This is not true, because the being a receptacle of some common qualities may depend on a partial identity, without that thing which is characterised by some attributes being necessarily also characterised by some others,—as we see in the case of such cognitions as 'that is this same Devadatta,' 'that is I,' [where the 'Devadatta' of yesterday and to-day, and the 'I' viewed under similarly different circumstances, are respectively identified in spite of some peculiar attributes]. For the knowledge of the special characteristics, which distinguish certain given things, must cause certain exceptions and limitations, [thus the 'Devadatta' of to-day and yesterday, which are thus identified, are respectively distinguished by certain peculiar attributes of time and place].

"Then you hold that there can be the knowledge of identity by means of the indirect (or secondary) mention of a thing [without its distinguishing characteristics]."[1] I reply, No,

[1] The direct meaning of a word is called 'denotation' (*abhidhá*); when this direct and principal meaning is incompatible with the rest of the sentence, we must have recourse to the indirect power of 'indication' (*lakshaṇá*). Thus in the sentence 'a herd-station on the Ganges,' the primary meaning of Ganges is incompatible, and therefore we reject the direct meaning (*abhidheya*) and take the indirect or secondary one (*lakshya*) of something connected with the river, as its bank. So here the Devadatta of to-day and yesterday are evidently distinct, and they cannot be absolutely identical, as they would be, if the words were to be accepted in their primary meaning; 'Devadatta' is therefore taken in its secondary meaning as viewed apart from the time, etc., in connexion with which he is spoken of. It is this residue of separate properties peculiar to each, as time, space, etc., which is the distinguishing characteristic (*avachhedaka*) which here establishes the relation *lakshyatá*.

because knowledge by means of indirect or secondary mention is always of an inferior kind [to that given by means of direct mention or *abhidhá*] and because it is only the presence of the distinguishing mark of this relation (*avachhedaka*) which causes the knowledge of the thing thus indirectly indicated.[1] Otherwise we might sometimes have the recollection of the thing directly denoted by a word (*abhidheya*) without the distinguishing mark which determines its being thus directly denoted [for the relations of *abhidheyatá* and *alakshyatá* equally require the presence of an *avachhedaka*].

Nor could the Supreme One be considered as subject to affliction, because a difference would be seen immediately after [the prima facie identity]. (33).

Nor can it be objected that, if this were so [*i.e.* if the individual and Supreme Soul were identical], the Supreme Being might be also defined as possessing affliction, etc., which belong to [the internal organ] the accidental disguiser of the individual soul; because, after the aforesaid recognition of their identity, there would follow the especial determination that all affliction, etc., were distinct from Soul.

If you say 'the same holds of power,'—no, because it is natural [to the Supreme]. (34).

"But would it not follow that power, defined by making, etc., would be excluded from the Supreme Being, just as afflictions and the like are; whereas the abstract quality of

[1] Every case of such a relation as *abhidheyatá, lakshyatá*, etc., must have an *avachhedaka* or determining notion which will be present to characterize it. In *abhidheyatá* this will be the divine will or (according to others) *sanketa*, 'human convention;' this determines the special meanings of different words, and is therefore called *pravṛitti-nimittam*; in *lakshyatá* this will be the special circumstances which cause an incompatibility between the primary meaning of the word and the rest of the sentence. In this last case it is these special circumstances which produce the knowledge of the secondary meaning. Thus in the sentence 'a herd-station on the Ganges' it is the idea of the river's surface, as incompatible with a solid house, which suggests the secondary meaning 'on the river's bank.'

power, viewed as residing in the soul [apart from all action], is not like affliction, etc." We deny it, because making, etc., are natural to the Supreme Being. The naturalness of heat to fire cannot be altered; therefore it is non-naturalness which constitutes the accidental. Therefore in the case of the sun as reflected in a mirror, we may exclude from the original the foulness which we detect in the image, [as this is only accidental;] but we cannot exclude the roundness, brightness, etc., which are natural to the sun.

"But is not the power of the Supreme Being real; how then can affliction, etc., be foreign [and accidental] to individual souls?" He proceeds to account for this.

The power of the Supreme is not disputed; and it is not thus in the case of the souls other than He, because they have his nature. (35).

The power of the Supreme is not denied in any Veda, that such a generally received belief should be held untenable. Rather we learn that power is natural to him from such passages as that in the Chhándogya Upanishad, "he whose will is truth," etc. Nor is there in his case any reason for his abandoning attributes once known to belong to him, as we hold that there is to individual souls, since he is always the Lord and always liberated. But affliction, etc., are not thus natural to the individual souls other than God,—why? because they have his nature. For we read in the Chhándogya Upanishad (viii. 3), "he attains to the supreme light and appears in his own nature," etc., and this would be impossible, if affliction, etc., were natural to the individual souls. It would indeed be possible if affliction, etc., were natural to the Supreme also, but this is not so. Therefore we conclude, because liberation, as defined as becoming identified with Brahman, would otherwise be impossible, that mundane existence [with its inevitable afflictions] is only accidental to embodied souls. Although Máyá is a non-natural power of the Supreme, still it does not follow that this his disguise will ever be absolutely abolished; but the internal organs, which are the disguisers of the individual souls, will be absolutely abolished, wherever faith is produced towards the Supreme. The Máyá-power of God never ceases, because, as the number of individual souls is infinite, its exercise by him is ever necessary, for their mundane existence and manifold service. And therefore such passages as those in the Śruti (Bṛihad Áraṇy. Upan. iv. 3, 7), "he as it were thinks, he as it were moves," etc., and again (Ib. ii. 3, 6), "hence there is this definition, 'he is not this,' 'he is not this,' etc., refer to the individual soul, [not to Brahman.]

If you say, 'what [becomes of God's power] apart from all souls?' —not so, from the infinity of internal organs. (36).

"But even if the liberation of individual souls is only gradual, still when all internal organs are abolished, the disguiser of the Supreme [his Máyá-power] will necessarily surcease, from the absence of all reason for its continuance; and then what becomes of the power which you have called natural to God?" We demur, for, as the number of internal organs which disguise the individual souls is infinite, such a time will never come; and so our view still remains reasonable that power is natural to God. Nor can we conclude that such a time will arrive, from the maxim "all antecedent non-existences[1] produce their opposites from the very fact of their being antecedent non-existences,"—[because the number of souls is infinite.] Nor can you say that all the antecedent non-existences will eventually have produced their opposites, because there is nothing to necessitate its being so. And there is an utter absence of argument to establish the probability of a time devoid of all effects; otherwise you might hold that there once was a time when *no* antecedent non-existence had as yet produced its opposite, and consequently infer a time when there

[1] I suppose there is here the tacit assumption that all individual souls have a prágabháva of mukti. (Prágabháva is the non-existence of a jar before it is made.)

was as yet no destruction [or emergent non-existence].[1] If you say that "such an idea as the possibility of my being one of the unfortunate souls who may never be liberated, would cut the sinews of effort towards liberation," I should reply that rather there would be every reason for effort, if there is a certainty as to what are the means, though uncertainty as to the attainment of the end; and on the other hand, it would be rather the idea that all will be certainly liberated, which would really lead to a paralysis of effort.

"If by the power which is natural to the Supreme, you mean the productive power of a material cause, then it will follow that the Supreme must be subject to change, just as clay (the material cause of jars) is." We reply

Brahman is not subject to change since matter is interposed as a screen,[2] following Him as He exists as thought. (37).

Matter is the material cause of inanimate effects, and is subject to change; but not so Brahman; the creative power of the Supreme is really through the development of himself and his being obeyed by matter. Nor can it be said that matter alone is existence, because this supposition would lead to individual souls being non-existent, as they are other than matter. Therefore we hold that creative power, etc., belong naturally to the Supreme, and that he throws a veil before himself in the form of his máyá-power or matter, [on which he works]; and therefore he himself is not subject to change, just as a magician who seems to create by illusion is not himself the subject of illusion.[3] Although [as the Sánkhyas say] the very fact of being an effect means being changed, since the cause and the effect are in their substrate identical, yet [when God creates] it is not such a change as involves a change of form, as in the

[1] The true view is that the succession of mundane existence (*saṃsára*) is eternal *à parte ante* and *à parte post*.

[2] Matter (*prakṛiti*) acts as a screen and stops the influence of change on Brahman.

[3] In p. 27, l. 7, the Sansk. Coll. MS. reads *-vikáryo* for *-káryo*.

case of milk becoming curds. Or again, we may say that God is not subject to change any more than the potter's stick is in reference to the jar,[1] since the stick does not effect any change in itself besides that produced in the jar. Therefore it is said in the Aphorism 'since matter is interposed as a screen.'

"But if Illusion is the material cause, is not the world founded upon illusion? How then can we find it declared by Śruti,—as in the passage,[2] 'on Him is all founded,'—that the world is founded on Brahman?" He answers as follows:

There is (still) the being founded upon Him, as in the case of a stool in a house. (38).

There is no contradiction in holding that the developments [of illusion] are also founded upon Him, Brahman, 'as in the case of a stool in a house;' *i.e.* just as one, standing on a stool placed in the middle of a house, is said equally to stand on the stool or in the house.

"But if so, is not Brahman rendered superfluous by our assumption of primeval Matter (*prakṛiti*)?" He denies this in the next aphorism.

Both [are needed] from their mutual dependence. (39).

Brahman and primeval Matter are both causes; since the intelligent and the non-intelligent mutually depend upon each other, the one for attaining self-knowledge and the other for attaining an object for its potentiality.[3] Which of them can ignore the other?[4]

He now proceeds to enumerate his categories, in order to facilitate the employment of the terms in his Śástra.

1 God in this view is the *instrumental* cause, and the potter's stick is not itself changed.

2 Taittiríya-khilopanishad, 26.

3 Cf. Sánkhya Káriká, 21.

4 In p. 28, l. 1, read किं कस्योपेचकं according to the Calcutta Sansk. Coll. MS. The printed text is nonsense.

There is no third beside 'knowable' and 'knower.'[1] (40).

The 'knowable' (*chetyá*) is 'Matter,' the 'knower' (*chit*) is Brahman; there is no other third thing; such is the meaning. If you say that this third thing need not be taken any account of,[2] as it is neither proved nor disproved,—we reply that what the Aphorism means is this: the state of knowing abides in none but Brahman, that of being knowable in nothing but Matter.

"But if there is no connexion between the Soul and matter, all effects are abolished; and if there is any connexion, then this itself will be the third." He answers,

And these two are joined from their being beginningless. (41).

'Mutually' must be supplied from Aph. 39, *i.e.* 'mutually joined.' Both these, previously mentioned, *i.e.* Soul and Matter, themselves constitute the connexion between them,[3] and we need not assume any extraneous connexion. Why? from their both being beginningless. And so it is said in the Gítá (xiii. 19),

"Know that Matter and Soul are both beginningless."

"Well then, let this very 'beginningless'[4] form the needed connexion between them." We demur, for, as the alternative lies between 'conscious' and 'unconscious,' the two terms do not admit of a third.

[Here follows a digression.] "But if Matter is only an illusion,—as is declared in the Śwetáśwatara and other Upanishads,

'Let him know that Matter is illusion, and Maheśwara the illusion-lord,'

does it not follow that Matter is all false? and if so, how is it described as the Category, 'what is to be known'?" He replies:

'What is to be known' is not false, from its being a power. (42).

1 Sc. 'object' and 'subject' (*chetyá* and *chit*).
2 For a somewhat similar example of this rare use of *chodyam*, cf. Mágha, ix. 16.
3 *i.e.* it is the so-called *swarúpa-sambandha* (cf. Kusumánjali, transl. p. 13, note).
4 Read p. 28, l. 14, *anádi eva* with Sansk. Coll. Lib. MS.

'What is to be known,' *i.e.* Matter, cannot be false,—why? 'from the very fact of its being a power.' Thus the magician cannot create the required extraneous thing without an illusive power. And again, in such passages as that, "but how, gentle youth, could the existent be thus born from the non-existent?" (Chhánd. Upan. vi. 2), the Śruti proves the reality of the cause from the reality of the effect, and so declares the reality, not the falseness of all. But we may also put the matter into the form of a regular inference; the divine Creation always depends upon a corresponding concomitant cause,[1] from the very fact of its being a creation made by an intelligent being,—just like the [illusive] creation of a magician. Nor may you say that "this argument is irrelevant, as all we want is gained by assuming *adṛishṭa*, etc.," because it is simpler to make one assumption, as we do in assuming this 'power,' and also because there is no proof that *adṛishṭa* is a cause of anything except experience and the means of producing it.[2] Again, since these other causes would inevitably overlap, if we tried to regard them as producing all effects [each being only partial in its operation], we consider that the existence of this máyá-power as the one eternal concomitant [to the Deity] is established. And as the further assumption of many other concomitants subordinate to this one is useful for the proposed end, it involves no real violation of the well-known law of parcimony. All this will be discussed at length in the third chapter.

The topic thus started as a digression being thus dismissed, our author returns to his original subject.

The purity of the faith is to be inferred from signs, as we see in common life. (43).

Although faith is an object of consciousness, through such

[1] The world resembles the máyá power of Íśwara.

[2] Thus it is said in the Kusumánjali (i. 12) "'the perceptible form, etc., and their absence (in ice and air) arise from contact with special causes,' and these special causes are the various kinds of merits in the person gratified by the cold air or ice."

cognitions as 'I have faith in (such a person),' 'I am devoted (to him),' etc., just as is the case with such cognitions as 'I know,' 'I wish,' etc.; still its 'purity,'—*i.e.* its being characterized by very strong impressions,—cannot be ascertained by direct consciousness, any more than the authoritativeness of knowledge can.[1] Therefore it can be ascertained only by certain observed signs,[2] 'as we see in common life.' Just as 'in common life' the greater or less degrees of affection must be inferred from the way that the person is affected at discourse concerning the loved object, etc., as by horripilation, tears, or other signs of emotion, so it is here.

But not only are there 'signs' as in common life, but these signs have been abundantly defined in the authoritative traditions (*smṛiti*) of the great sages; so the author declares as follows:

And we learn from the Smṛitis such signs in abundance, as respect, honour, joy, forlornness, doubt as to any other object, celebration of his praise, continuing to live for his sake, considering everything as his, regarding him as being in all things, resignation to his will, etc. (44).

i. 'Respect,' as that shown by Arjuna (Mahábh. Droṇa parva, l. 2822), "The righteous winner of wealth, in whatever posture he may be, never fails to rise up before Kṛishṇa, with faith and affection."

ii. 'Honour,' as that of Ikshwáku (Nṛisiṃha Pur. xxv. 22), "Through his fondness for his name, and for the deer and lotus

[1] The Prábhákara school of the Mímáṃsá hold that knowledge is an object of internal perception, and its correctness (or authoritativeness, *prámáṇya*) is cognised by the same act of cognition as the knowledge itself. There is 1. the perception of the object, *i.e.* 'this is a jar;' 2. the consciousness of this perception, *i.e.* 'I perceive the jar;' 3. simultaneously with (2) the cognition of the truth of the perception. The Nyáya holds that the three steps are successive, and the last is gained by inference, not by direct consciousness. If it were gained by direct consciousness, there could be no such thing as doubt.

[2] The Sansk. Coll. MS. reads ज्ञात- for जात- in p. 29, l. 17.

which resembled him, the king showed honour even to the cloud which was of the same [blue] colour [as Kṛishṇa]."

iii. 'Joy' as that of Vidura (Mahábh. Udyoga P. lxxxviii.); "The joy which I feel because of thy coming, O lotus-eyed, why should it be told to thee? thou art the inmost soul of all embodied beings."

iv. 'Forlornness,' as that of the milkmaids (Vishṇu Pur. V. xviii.), "It is not possible for us to speak before our parents,—what can I say? What can our parents do for us burned with the fire of absence?"

v. 'Doubt as to any other object,' as, for instance, the feeling of hindrance in the minds of the dwellers in Śwetadwípa, even at the sight of the divine sage Nárada[1] (Mahábh. Śánti P. l. 12883); or as that of Upamanyu (Mahábh. Anuśásana P. l. 7077), "At Śankara's command I would be even a worm or a grasshopper; but I desire not even the three worlds, if given, Indra, by thee."

vi. 'Celebration of his praise,' as that by Yama (Nṛisiṃha P. viii. 21), "The guilty one, tormented in hell, was thus addressed by Yama, 'Why is not the god Keśava, the destroyer of sorrow, worshipped by thee?'"

Or, again, (Vishṇu P. III. vii.), "Having seen his emissary with noose in hand, Yama thus whispers in his ear, 'Spare those who take refuge in Madhusúdana; I am lord of other men, but not of Vaishṇavas.'"

vii. 'Continuing to live for his sake,' as in Hanumat's case (Rámáyaṇa, Utt. Káṇḍa, cvii.), "As long as thy purifying story shall circulate through the world, so long will I remain on the earth, obeying thy command."

[1] Nárada goes to S'wetadwípa, a region inhabited by intense monotheists who worship only Vishṇu. The god shows himself to him and then bids him at once depart to his home: "These my votaries, filled with faith in me, ceasing from their five senses and from food, and brilliant as the moon, would fain fix all their thoughts on me; let there be no hindrance to their wish."

Or as in the continuance in life of Nárada and others, though they had accomplished all their ends, solely for the sake of adoring him. Hence we have that passage of Śruti (Nṛisiṃha-tápaní, vi.), "He whom all the gods worship desiring liberation, and the reciters of the Veda."

viii. 'Considering everything as his,' as in the case of the Vasu Uparichara (Mahábh. Śánti P. cccxxxvii.), "His kingdom, and his wealth, his wife and his chariot,—he regards them always as all belonging to Bhagavat."

ix. 'Regarding him as being in all things,' as in the well-known case of Prahláda; as for instance his words (Vishṇu P. I. xix.), "Thus an unwavering love for all beings is to be cherished by those sages who know that Hari is all things."

x. 'Resignation to his will,' as of Bhíshma, even when Bhagavat approached to kill him (Mahábh. Bhíshma P. lviii.), "Come, lord of the gods, home of the world,—adoration to thee, bearing in thy hand bow, club, and sword,—slay me by force, O ruler of the world, from thy chariot, O thou refuge of living beings in battle."[1]

By the word. 'etc.' we are also referred to the actions of Uddhava, Akrúra, etc.[2] Although this has been already mentioned in Aphorism 6, 'It is an affection from its being the opposite of hatred,' still there is a distinction between the two places, as there the intention was to give a sign to denote the presence of affection, while here it is to give a sign of the purity of faith.

"But do we not see hatred, jealousy, etc., felt by those who are devotedly attached to their lord towards those who experience a greater degree of his favour; why then should not these also be considered as signs?" He replies,

[1] I have followed in the last line the reading of the Calcutta printed text, as that given in the S'áṇḍilya Comm. seems to be corrupt.

[2] Uddhava was Kṛishṇa's cousin, see Wilson's *Vishṇu P.* (Hall's ed. vol. iv. p. 113); Akrúra was Kṛishṇa's uncle on the father's side.

But hatred, etc., are not so. (45).

I.e. from their incompatibility, as has been said by the venerable Dwaipáyana (Mahábh. Anúsána P. cxlix.),

"Neither anger, nor envy, nor greed, nor impure thoughts belong to the sanctified ones who are devoted to Purushottama."

While in the case of Śiśupála there is the following succession to be traced; from hatred arose continual remembrance, from that came the highest faith, and from that liberation.

"These 'signs,' however, are chiefly mentioned in the Smṛiti as having been produced in reference to Vishṇu's Avatáras, but this faith of yours should have reference to the Supreme since it springs from the knowledge of Brahman." He declares the true view.

From the implied remainder of the sentence this [faith] is also directed towards manifestations [as in an avatára]. (46).

This highest faith may also have as its object an avatára itself,[1] as is seen 'from the implied remainder of the sentence.' [He proceeds to explain this.] It is said (Gítá, vii. 23),

"The worshippers of the gods go to the gods, those who have faith in me go likewise to me."

Here, in order to enforce the main point, there is an implied meaning of censure of the faith directed towards other deities. Therefore, in the passage (vii. 21),

"Whatever form any one devoted wishes to worship with faith, to him I make that very faith unwavering;"

as the sense would have been complete, if the words had run "whatever (deity) any one, etc.," we infer, from the addition of the word 'form,' that the real meaning must be that this faith has as its object the avatára itself [and thus refers to Vishṇu's own assumed forms]. The entire topic is faith.

[1] I take *átman* in *prádurbháváman* as meaning 'itself;' but it might mean 'the soul manifested in an *avatára*.' Cf. l. 13, and p. 37, l. 10.

From revelation we learn that there is no further birth to him who knows (His) births and actions. (47).

His 'births,'—*i.e.* Bhagavat's assuming a body for the performance of those effects to which a body is indispensable, as being visible to his votaries, slaying the demons, producing the Veda, etc. His 'actions,' *i.e.* his producing the Veda, etc. To him who knows these aright, [this knowledge] leads to immunity from all future births; as He himself declares (Gítá, iv. 9),

"My birth and my action are divine; whosoever knows thus in truth, he, on abandoning the body, is born no more, but goes to me, Arjuna."

Not that immortality is the direct fruit of this knowledge of His births and actions; but, by abolishing the foulness of that mind which is fixed on these, it produces the highest faith having for its object the supreme Íśwara as conditioned by these *avatáras*, and so leads to the immunity from all future births. Therefore we maintain that Revelation itself allows that the being who assumes an *avatára* may be the object of the highest faith.

And these are divine from their being produced solely by his own power. (48).

What does the 'divine' character mean in those words of the Gítá just quoted, "my birth and my action are divine"? It cannot mean that they are produced by reason of previous merit, because there is in him no contact with merit, as 'consequences of actions' are not proved to belong to him. Nor can it mean their being produced in heaven, because then the character would not apply, when (as in the case of Kṛishṇa) the birth is in the world of our earth. Rather it means that here there is no making use of any gross material cause as in the case of the ordinary body; but it is all [directly] produced by his own máyá power. Hence we have those words of Bhagavat to Nárada in the 'Liberation' book [of the Mahábhárata, cccxli.],

"All this is a máyá created by me, that thou seest me at all, Nárada."

And so too in the Gítá (iv. 6),

"Though myself unborn, of an eternal nature, and lord of all beings, yet making use of my subject Nature, I am born from æon to æon."

Nor is the circumstance that his body is not composed of the gross elements any bar to its being a body,—since its being composed of the gross elements is only necessary so far as it is to be the seat of the enjoyment of the fruits of former actions [and these, as we just now said, are out of the question in regard to Kṛishṇa]. If you say that its being such a seat of enjoyment is essential to the idea of a body,—I reply that it is simpler to hold that the true idea of a body is its being the seat of voluntary effort. Effort is a particular species of the genus 'action'; for we must not say that effort is the same as action, or we should have to apply the term to the forced movements of a dead body [under the influence of magic].[1] Nor may we say that effort is action produced by direct volition,—because then it would follow that we ought to apply such a phrase as 'it makes an effort' to a pot, since all acts [as of a pot's boiling its contents] are produced by the direct volition of Íśwara. Now the same argument which proves Íśwara to have a body establishes the efforts produced by that body, and so the discussion may rest here.

Nor does it follow that, if we thus grant the existence of such a body for Kṛishṇa, we must raise the number of principles or 'primary existences' [to 27 instead of 26, as this body will be quite *sui generis;*] because it will not be a 'principle' at all, any more than a common effect is, as a pot, etc.,—since neither of them acts as the material cause of any external object which

[1] Cf. the scene of the old witch and her slain son in the sixth book of Heliodorus' *Æthiopica*; or *kriyá* may mean such actions as the dead body's falling to the ground, etc. I prefer this to taking *mṛitaśaríra-kriyá* as 'the last offices paid to a dead body,' which would simply be a quibble on the word *kriyá*.

helps to make up the visible world; nor again does it act as the material cause of the senses.[1]

"But how does He act, as He has no object to move Him?" He replies,

His chief object indeed is compassion. (49).

In common life we apply the term 'compassionate' to those who exert themselves for the disinterested[2] removal of others' sorrow. But this is not the highest application of the word, since these persons are not entirely disinterested in their action, as they may act in order to avoid the pain caused by their sense of pity or in order to attain subsequent merit. Nor, again, would its highest application be right in the case of any one who merely acts to remove others' sorrow,[3] since we do not apply it to one who has ulterior objects in view by so doing, as *e.g.* gaining wealth, etc. But the compassion of Bhagavat is compassion in its highest sense, when He disinterestedly abolishes others' woe. For His sake we use the term 'compassionate' in only a secondary sense, when we apply it to those who aim at other objects. Hence we say that men act from their feeling

[1] S'áṇḍilya holds that Kṛishṇa is really a form of the Supreme Brahman (see Comm. on Aph. 52); but his body is not a separate primary principle (*tattwa*) from the acknowledged 26 of the Vedánta, as it is not a tattwa at all. The 26 tattwas are divided first into two great classes, as intelligent (*chit*) and non-intelligent (*achit*). The former includes I's'wara and the individual soul, the second all the rest. But the second is in turn similarly divided into general (*vyápaka*) and special (*vyápya*); the special are the five elements, the five tanmátras and the eleven senses and organs; the general are matter (*i.e.* I's'wara's máyá power), intellect and egoism (see Comm. on Aph. 87). The special spring from the general, as their material cause; and in turn themselves produce all the different individual existences (as pots, etc.) in the world. But the divine body of Kṛishṇa is not like the special tattwas, as nothing in the gross world springs from it; nor can it be like the general tattwas, because these are the material cause of the elements, senses, organs, etc., but this divine body is not the material cause of anything. (Cf. the Tattwa-kaumudí in its Comm. on Sánkhya-káriká, aphorism 3, where it is shown that such effects, as pots, etc. cannot be called *tattwas*.)

[2] Perhaps *nirupddhi* in p. 35, l. 3, should be corrected to *nirupadhi* 'genuine,' 'guileless;' *nirupádhi* however means pretty much the same thing, 'unconditioned,' 'disinterested.'

[3] *i.e.* omitting the word 'disinterested' from our previous definition.

of compassion, having regard at the same time to the merit which the action will produce.

"But might we not say that, as all pre-eminent manifestations of power are said in the Gítá to be forms of Bhagavat (according to the line, 'know me to be also amongst men the king,' etc., Gítá, x. 27), liberation might also follow from faith directed towards a king, etc?" He replies,

It is not directed towards pre-eminent manifestations of power, because they have to do with the vital airs. (50).

The highest form of faith is directed only to a Being unassociated with the individual soul; but when faith[1] is directed towards such beings as kings and others, who are connected with the vital airs, etc., which are the disguisers of the individual soul, it cannot have liberation as its fruit.

And because of the prohibition of gambling and the king's service. (51).

We read in the Dharmáśástras that gambling and the king's service are both prohibited;[2] but this would not be so, if the king were [the same as] the Supreme Being [and so a proper object for faith].

If you say 'this also applies to Vásudeva,'—no, because he is the real form (of Brahman). (52).

"But when the Śruti speaks of these pre-eminent manifestations of power, does it not mention among them 'I am Vásudeva among the Vṛishṇis' (Gítá, x. 37), and therefore [as the manifestation as Vásudeva here only runs parallel to that as a king, etc., in x. 27,] it would follow that the manifestation as Vásudeva is no more to be an object of faith than the others?" We cannot admit this, because the Supreme Brahman is really in the form of Kṛishṇa; as Paráśara says (Vishṇu Pur. IV. xi.),

[1] In p. 35, l. 15, read भक्तिः for रक्तिः.

[2] I do not know the exact verse here referred to, but the sentiment is found in Böhtlingk's *Indische Sprüche* (2nd ed.), 2992, 2995.

"If a man hears the line of the race of Yadu, he is delivered from all sins, that race in which the Supreme Brahman became incarnate as a man, under the name of Kṛishṇa."
This would not be so, if Kṛishṇa were only an individual soul.

And from his recognition as such. (53).

We find in Śruti a distinct recognition of the son of Vasudeva as the Supreme Brahman, as (in the Náráyaṇa Upanishad, Atharva Śiras, vi.)[1]

"The son of Devakí is related to Brahman, the destroyer of Madhu is related to Brahman;
"There is one form of the Supreme Brahman belonging to Náráyaṇa, pervading all beings, existing as the cause (of all), itself uncaused." And this same recognition is also found in Smṛiti, as in the words to Yudhishṭhira, uttered by Márkaṇḍeya, who had had ocular experience of a mundane destruction[2] (Mahábh. Vana Parva, clxxxix.),

"That god who was beheld by me of old, having eyes long as a lotus-petal, is now, O tiger of men, thine own relation, Janárdana."

So too (Mahábh. Śánti P. cccxlv.) Janamejaya says, after hearing that Bhagavat is not to be seen even by force of penances,

"He who is not to be seen even by force of penances, Bhagavat worshipped by the world,—him they have seen visibly manifested, adorned with the Śrívatsa mark."

The 'and' in the Aphorism implies that another reason is found in the fact that the Smṛiti expressly mentions a reward to those who are devoted to him.

"How then is it that we find Vásudeva himself enumerated among the pre-eminent manifestations of power [as in the Gítá, x. 37]?" He replies,

That is to be explained by his superiority among the Vṛishṇis. (54).

In such passages as 'I am Vishṇu among the A'dityas,'

[1] Compare Weber, Indische Stud. ii. p. 54.
[2] He is called *Sapta-kalpánta-jívanaḥ*, "living through seven æon-destructions."

(Gítá, x. 21) this mention of him among the pre-eminent manifestations of power is simply to show that Parameśwara has the superiority amongst *them;* and so too this similar mention of Vásudeva (in x. 37) is simply intended to show that he is the superior among the Vṛishṇis.

And so too with regard to other well-known [similar manifestations]. (55).

In the same way we are to infer that faith will produce liberation as its fruit, when it is directed towards the boar, man-lion, dwarf, Ráma, and other *avatáras,* which are well known to possess, like the Vásudeva *avatára,* the signs of the supreme Brahman. Or the aphorism may mean that we are to understand a similar meaning of mere superiority over the other pre-eminent manifestations of power, which are well known to possess the signs of the Supreme Brahman, as *e.g.* "I am also Śankara among the Rudras," etc. It is said in the Skánda Puráṇa (Káśí-khaṇḍa, i. § 27),

"He who would declare that there is any distinction between Vishṇu and Rudra or between Śrí and Gaurí,—that utterance of that erring fool is blamed by the Śástra."

The fact that Śankara *is* well known to possess the signs of Brahman, is abundantly to be recognized as taught in the Smṛiti, etc.

Thus ends the first daily portion of the second Chapter of the Commentary on the Hundred Aphorisms of Śáṇḍilya, composed by the most learned teacher Swapneśwara.

The two manifest aids to faith, knowledge and devout concentration (*yoga*), have been discussed; the author now proceeds to discuss the inferior forms of faith, which have final bliss attached to them in an indirect way, inasmuch as they destroy the sin which would hinder its attainment.

Since 'bhajana' is summed up in 'bhakti,' the lower[1] *form exists for the higher as it is a means to its production.* (56).

The Gítá, after praising the highest form of faith as set forth in the seventh chapter, by the line (ix. 13),

"Having known me as the imperishable, the first of beings, they worship me (*bhajanti*) with undiverted minds;"

proceeds to notice [the inferior forms] in the next couplet,

"Always reciting my names and striving, firm in their vow,
And paying homage with faith (*bhakti*), they serve me, perpetually devoted;"

and after that (in ch. ix. 29) we have the summing up of the whole subject in the words,

"But they who worship me (*bhajanti*) with faith (*bhakti*), are in me and I in them."

Now with regard to this passage, just as the Mímáṃsakas explain the text "let him sacrifice with *chitrá*" (Taitt. Saṃh. ii. 4, 6),[2] so here we must take it as meaning, "let him produce the desired fruit by worship (*bhajana*), which is expressed by the term *bhakti*," and in this way the fruit [bliss,] and the habit of mind [worship,] will be both found residing in the same subject. [If you ask why the author of the Gítá used the word *bhakti* when he meant *bhajana*, we reply that] the word *bhakti* came ready to the author's hand as having been already used of the habit of mind towards Bhagavat in such

1 I read गौणी for गौण्या with the Sanksrit Coll. Library MS.

2 This alludes to a Mímáṃsá discussion on the text "let him who desires cattle, sacrifice with the *chitrá*." A discussion is raised (Nyáya-málá-vistara, i. 4. 3) as to the meaning of *chitrá*,—is it merely the name of a sacrifice, so called from the six various objects, honey, ghee, etc., offered in it; or does it mean the spotted she-goat which is the Agníshomíya victim? The Mímáṃsá decides that *chitrá* here means the name of the sacrifice; as in this way the desired fruit (cattle) and the prescribed means (the *chitrá* sacrifice) will both belong to (or reside in) the same subject, the offerer. If it had meant the spotted she-goat used as a victim in the Agníshomíya sacrifice, then in the words "let him who desires cattle sacrifice with the spotted she-goat," the fruit would have belonged to the sacrificer, but the spotted she-goat would have been a characteristic of the sacrifice, and belonged to it, and thus we should have had *vaiyadhikaraṇya*.

passages as "he who has faith in one (*ekabhaktiḥ*) is pre-eminent" (vii. 17); and moreover *bhakti* and *bhajana* are originally synonymous [being similar derivatives from the root *bhaj*].

We must not say that the highest form of *bhakti* is here enjoined as producing the fruit of supreme bliss,—because we have already seen in Aphorism 7 that the highest form of faith cannot be thus enjoined by rule, as it is not to be produced by a mere effort of human will. Nor again can we say, that the fact of its being a cause of supreme bliss was before unknown and is now first definitely declared in the Gítá,—because this fact had been already declared in the seventh chapter by the words "they who have faith in me go likewise to me." The true view is rather that these ceremonial repetitions of a deity's names, etc., were originally only brought in with a view to show that they were means for removing the hindrances to the highest faith; but afterwards the word *bhakti* in the instrumental case was applied to them in a secondary sense [in ix. 14], and thus they were enjoined as themselves means to produce the highest faith. We are thus led to the closing passage (in ix. 29), "They are in me and I am in them," as a 'persuasive enforcement,' giving the purpose of this injunction (*arthaváda*).—Otherwise we should have had to divide the sentence, and to read it, "by *bhakti* they attain *bhajana*, and by this they dwell in me."

As such acts as repeating a deity's names, etc., are a means for producing faith in the worshipper's soul, the word '*bhakti*' is used here in a secondary sense which is easily understood from the literal one, just as in the Vaidic phrase "ghee verily is life" [where the real meaning is not that ghee is literally itself 'life,' but that it is a great means for prolonging it]. Or the word *bhakti* may be applied to these ceremonies, as meaning that they are instruments of worship, *i.e.* "he is worshipped by these things" (*bhajyate ebhiḥ*); just as the word *udbhid* [is applied to a particular kind of sacrifice, as well as to a shovel, from its etymological meaning *udbhidyate paśuphalam anena* 'the desired fruit, sc. cattle, is dug up by it.'][1] Or the term may be used from our reading in the Gítá of the various grades of worship, "four several kinds of men worship me" (vii. 16),—so that the term itself implies 'varieties' as the term 'creation' does. Or it may be a secondary sense of the term as characterized by the vague and less discriminating attribute 'noble-minded,' since we read in the Gítá (vii. 18) "all these are noble-minded, but the knower I hold as myself."

And since the other [inferior forms of faith] are associated with the recitation of the god's names as tending to stir up affection. (57).

It is said in the Gítá (xi. 36),

"Well is the world, O lord of the senses, delighted and filled with love at thy praises."

Here we have it directly affirmed that the recital of the deity's names is for the purpose of stirring up feelings of affection.—"Since they are associated with it," all the other observances which are mentioned with 'recitation' in the Gítá (ix. 14, etc.)—"always reciting my names and striving firm in their vow," etc.—will also have as their end the production of affection [*i.e.* faith] in the soul.

But the inferior forms are mentioned in the interval; and they are also alluded to in the Vedic references to objects of adoration, from the very fact that they are found in the Brahmakáṇḍa. (58).

The inferior forms of faith which are mentioned in the Gítá between the two aforesaid passages, "Having known me as the imperishable, the first of beings, they worship me with undiverted minds" (ix. 13), and "But they who worship me with faith are in me and I in them" (ix. 29),—are really subsidiary to the highest faith, being included as by nippers between two

[1] Dr. Ballantyne, in his edition of the text, gives a reference here to Áśwaláyana's S'rauta-sútras; but the true reference is rather to the derivation of *udbhid* suggested in the Mímáṃsá, compare Jaiminíya-Nyáya-málá-vistara, i. 4. 2.

distinct mentions of this highest faith. Thus we read (in ix. 14, 15, 22, 25–28) as follows,

"Always reciting my names and striving firm in their vow, and paying homage with faith, they serve me perpetually devoted. And others serve me, sacrificing with the sacrifice of knowledge, and worshipping me in unity or in plurality, or as facing every way in many guises."

"They who serve and think on me, with their minds fixed on nought besides,—to them, ever devoted to me, I bring sure bliss."

"Those devoted to the gods go to the gods, those devoted to the ancestors go to the ancestors, those who sacrifice to goblins go to the goblins, and those also who sacrifice to me go to me. He who gives to me with faith a leaf, a flower, a fruit, or water,—I eat it from him pure-souled as offered in faith. Whatever thou doest, whatever thou eatest, whatever thou offerest, whatever thou givest, whatever penance thou undergoest, O son of Kuntí,—give it all over to me. Thus shalt thou be delivered from all good or evil consequences, caused by works."

Here 'recitation' means repeating the deity's names; and worldly 'striving' also to attain faith is likewise mentioned with it, as the subject-matter is the different subsidiary helps to faith. 'Firmness in their vow,' *i.e.* their performing through faith in me such ceremonial observances as the fasting on the eleventh lunar day,[1] etc. 'Paying homage' (*namaskára*), *i.e.* the performance of such ceremonies as the raising the hands to the head in token of self-abasement. The 'sacrifice of knowledge' is twofold, the superior and the inferior, as directed respectively to unity or plurality. The 'thinking on Him alone' is the contemplation and continual remembrance of Him. 'Sacrifice'

[1] "Every eleventh lunar day is held in extravagant veneration by the Hindus, but more particularly by the Vaishṇavas. Fasting on the eleventh day is declared to be equally efficacious with a thousand aśwamedhas, and eating during its continuance as heinous a sin as parricide or the murder of a spiritual teacher."—Wilson's *Essays on the Religions of the Hindus*, vol. ii. p. 204.

is worship directed to Bhagavat, and the giving of leaves, etc., and so, too, the giving over of all enjoined or forbidden actions to the Supreme Lord.

These, however, are not the only subordinate helps; for other means to produce faith are hidden[1] in such passages about worship as that of the Chhándogya Upanishad (iii. 18), "let him adore the mind as Brahman," or that of the Gítá (x. 21), "I am Vishṇu among the Ádityas," etc. If you ask "why?" I answer that we are authorized to conclude so, because the whole of the Theosophical part of the Veda treats of faith or the means for its production in the soul.[2]

From these arises purification, as we see by the introduction of the subject. (59).

From these inferior forms of faith arises 'purification,' *i.e.* the removal of the sin which causes the foulness of the internal organ; this, however, is itself a means [not the end]. Why? because these inferior forms are mentioned in the Gítá, after introducing the subject (in ix. 2) by the words "this is the best purifier." Purification is an indispensable means, since faith is a quality of the internal organ [which is produced after purification has accomplished its preliminary work].[3]

Some infer a greater degree of fruit from this conjunction of the higher faith with these. (60).

Some teachers hold that the joint mention of the higher faith in connexion with these inferior forms, as the recitation of names, etc., in such passages as "he who offers to me with faith," (ix. 26), "paying homage to me with faith" (ix. 14), etc.,—as it is certain from the context, etc., that these latter forms must hold a subordinate position,—can only be in order to show that there is a higher degree of fruit to those who, having exercised their faith, also practise these lower observances.

[1] Literally 'swallowed up by.'

[2] Or as it was said in the Commentary on Aphorism 26, 'faith is the end of the brahma-káṇḍa.'

[3] Compare pp. 47, 52, *suprà.*

Jaimini thinks that it is only as a name, from the possibility. (61).

But the teacher Jaimini[1] (as the fact of these forms being inferior is certain) thinks that the same explanation holds here which holds in regard to the Vedic injunction "let him who is using a spell against an enemy sacrifice with the *śyena*." [Now it is shown in the Aphorisms of the Mímáṃsá that *śyena* does not mean there 'a hawk,' but is the special name of the ceremony;[2] and so Jaimini maintains that] the word 'faith' is only used in this passage of the Gítá in a subordinate way as a special name for the actions described, and thus the passage means "let him secure the highest faith by the [so-called special] faith, 'repeating the deity's names,' and by the [so-called special] faith 'giving'"—since in this way we have the possibility of their all referring to the same subject;[3] and thus it will have no reference to any fruit of its own, which would only introduce a needless complication.

Here these subordinate means are to be performed according to time and opportunity, as in building a house, etc. (62).

Now three alternatives present themselves. The repetition of names, paying homage, and the other aforementioned observances, may be either performed simultaneously, or any one singly, or all in order. But we cannot accept the first alternative, because then we should have the whole failing, if any one observance were left unperformed; nor can we accept the second, because if there were thus an unlimited option, it would involve their all having one and the same use; and the third alternative will not suit the meaning of the text; and again, when one observance was performed, it would seem unnecessary trouble to perform the next. And therefore the primâ facie conclusion is that these different observances cause mutual confusion by each intruding into the province of the others.

[1] Is this an adaptation of Jaimini's doctrine (in Sút. i. 4. 5); or does it refer to a modern writer of that name?

[2] So called from its suddenly destructive effects on the enemy.

[3] *i.e.* they will be all alike instances of the lower faith, sc. means to the higher.

But the true conclusion is that all these observances are alike means [to produce faith], since all have authority for their being followed. But there is no necessity for the simultaneous performance of all, from the absence of any authority for it; those only need to be practised simultaneously, the simultaneous use of which is commanded in the Śruti, as perfumes, flowers, incense, lamps, oblations, etc. All the other observances may be performed according to time and opportunity, as in the making of a house, etc.; *i.e.* just as men bring the various materials for a house, as the thatch, pillars, etc., sometimes all at once and sometimes in succession; and it does not follow, however they may be brought, that the thatch, etc., cease to be means for the desired end. Therefore whatever sin each observance is specially suited to destroy, let it be performed for that purpose; and thus all having respectively shown their various efficacy, the highest faith will be eventually produced in the soul; and so it is declared in the Gítá (vii. 19),

"At the end of many births he who has knowledge attains me."

From pleasing the Supreme Lord even one may be effectual. (63).

Among these inferior means any one may become powerful by special practice, and this even by itself may produce pleasure in the Supreme Lord and so avail to cause the highest faith; just as we see that an earthly lord is not pleased by his other attendants with all their many careless services, but may be pleased by even one attendant with a simple act of shampooing performed with hearty zeal. The highest faith may be attained, through the favour of Bhagavat, by even one of these inferior means, as repetition of names, etc., resolutely carried out; as we read in the Gítá (xviii. 57),

"Devoting thyself to concentration of thought, fix thy mind on me; he whose mind is fixed on me will, by my favour, cross over all difficulties."

So too any particular one may have a peculiar efficacy derived from a certain time, etc., as it is said in such passages as the following [in the Brahma Puráṇa, ch. xcvii. 166],

"What one obtains by meditation in the Kṛita, by sacrifices in the Tretá, and by outward worship in the Dwápara, that one obtains in the Kali by merely reciting Keśava's name."

Nor will the different means interfere with each other, since recitation of the deity's names, and the other means, produce their respective influence by their own nature, in each individual case where faith is to be powerfully excited.

Is the purification [spoken of in Aphorism 59] the means [for obtaining the highest faith] in the case of all who are occupied with the recitation of names, etc., or is something else the means in the case of some? He replies:

That absence of bondage, which belongs to surrendering works, is the true means. (64).

The true means [for attaining the highest faith] is that absence of all bondage consisting in a cessation from all consequences, which arises in the case of those who have surrendered all their good and evil works to Bhagavat. As we read [in the Gítá, ix. 28],

"Thus thou shalt be delivered from good and evil consequences, caused by works."

And there is a formula for this surrender of our works in another Puráṇa,

"Whatever I do, good or evil, with or without my will,
That being all surrendered to thee, I do it as impelled by thee."

Nor would it follow in this way that a man might do as he pleased, under the pretence of acting as thus impelled by Him; because the absence of doing evil is really one part of this divine impulsion. And so the Smṛiti, "A man could not be devoted to sin, while depending on strength derived from the Veda." Therefore we say that this 'purification' must have for its object something other than doing evil. Now good deeds are to be understood as meaning the necessary and occasional observances[1] prescribed by one's period of life (*A'śrama*). The world of Brahmá, etc., is the reward attained by the due observance of the duties of one's *áśrama,* and the very attainment of this reward would delay the summum bonum, liberation; and therefore this and the like are called 'bondage' in the Aphorism. But when all is surrendered to Brahman, it is well known that it is a means to liberation. Thus, too, there is an absence of consequences when the voluntary works engaged in through desire of fruit, or evil works engaged in through ignorance, are afterwards surrendered [to Brahman].

But here we must consider a distinction in these subordinate forms of faith. Thus, for instance, we find a description like that [in the Chhándogya Upanishad, i. 6], "That golden male who is seen within the sun, with golden beard and golden hair," etc.; and so too [in the Nárada-pancharátra, xi. 71.],

"He is ever to be meditated on who resides within the orb of the sun, Náráyaṇa, seated on his lotus seat; crest-bearing, wearing bracelets and *makara* earrings, decked with a string of pearls, golden-formed, and carrying a conch and discus."

Is meditation to be restricted to these [special manifestations] or is it to be extended to the complete [formless] manifestations of the divine nature, as given in other śrutis? The primâ facie answer which suggests itself is that it is restricted by the śruti's mentioning the definite nature of the object to be thus meditated upon; but the following Aphorism supplies the true answer.

[1] Ceremonial works are of three kinds, 'constant,' 'occasional,' and 'voluntary.' The 'constant' are those continually enjoined through a Bráhman's life, as the daily and fortnightly offerings; the 'occasional' are enjoined on certain occasions, as recovery from sickness, an eclipse, etc.; the 'voluntary' are directed to some special end, as 'let him who desires heaven offer the jyotishṭoma.' It is generally held that the first two are positive duties and cannot be omitted without sin; but their performance does not produce bondage by causing merit in the offerer. The 'voluntary' offerings necessitate a future reward, and as they thus produce bondage, they should be avoided by the devotee. S'áṇḍilya, however, holds that even 'constant' and 'occasional' works, as well as 'voluntary,' produce 'merit,' and so tend to cause bondage, unless they are surrendered in faith to Iśwara.

But the [apparent] restriction of the meditation is given because of the easiness of a visible object. (65).

The reason why the Śruti mentions a particular object for one's meditation is in order to present the mind with some visible object, as the mind might become distracted by a variety of objects. Therefore its mention is to be considered as arising only because of the greater easiness,—as there might be the risk of an option and other difficulties, if the meditation were directed only to the unseen. Therefore the rule will be different in regard to different passages of Śruti. Hence we see that without some such definite mention the fruit of meditation would have been hard to obtain in the case of the milkmaids and Śiśupála, etc.

The root 'yaj' there means worship; not so in the other sacrifices. (66).

"In the Gítá (ix. 25) it is said 'those also who sacrifice to me (*mad-yájinaḥ*) go to me;' does the root *yaj*, used here, refer to the well-known *jyotishṭoma* and other offerings, or does it mean 'worship'?" We answer,—*yaj* is used here only in the sense of 'worship.' How is this known? By such injunctions as "let him worship Vishṇu," etc., necessary and voluntary worship is already expressly enjoined with reference to Vishṇu; and the Gítá only enjoins this 'worship' here as a subsidiary part of the highest faith,[1] and does not itself expressly enjoin that it should be performed with a reference to Vishṇu.[2] But in the case of the other offerings [*i.e.* the *jyotishṭoma*, etc.] we do not find any express declaration that they are directed to Vishṇu; in fact, in that case, we should be forced to divide the sentence of the Gítá, ["those who sacrifice to me, go to me,"] into two

[1] This refers to the Comm. on Aph. 58, where vv. 14–28 (Gítá, § ix.) are considered to refer to the ancillary forms of worship included (as 'between nippers') between vv. 13 and 29, which describe the higher form.

[2] I read in p. 45, l. 3, *na* for *tena*, as this is the reading of both MSS. in the Calcutta Sanskrit College Library.

distinct declarations, viz. one to establish that these sacrifices were directed to Vishṇu at all, the other that they were related to faith.—"Well then, [if an offering's connexion with Vishṇu is what gives it this relation], let us hold that there is this connexion with faith in such a special and voluntary offering as that prescribed in the text, 'he offers an oblation of milk and butter to the wide-stepping Vishṇu.'"[1] We concede this in part;—but the example you give is an imperfect one, since voluntary oblations [which are offered with a certain definite end] have properly no reference to any farther end when that immediate end is obtained; and I would rather exemplify this connexion with faith by the case of those constant daily offerings which the very fact of living makes obligatory [apart from any accidental desires, such as might prompt voluntary offerings]; since there is nothing to hinder this view,[2] and, inasmuch as they are constant, they are always at hand.

Hence in the Mokshadharma section of the Mahábhárata, we read, in the censure of acts of worship accompanied with injury to living beings (Mahábh. Śánti P. cclxvi.),[3]

"The righteous-souled Manu prescribed avoidance of injury in all ceremonial works; it is because men are filled with [unnecessary] desires that they slaughter the cattle outside the *Vedi*.[4] They alone who know Vishṇu worship him rightly, with offerings of milk and flowers; thus is his worship prescribed in the smṛiti."

Now follow three sections (*adhikaraṇas*) arising from the topic of *pújá* as just discussed.

1 This is some passage, describing an offering made to Vishṇu under a particular manifestation, and for some particular desired object. Although in the indicative mood, it appears to be considered as an imperative injunction, compare the Mímáṃsá discussion, Taitt. Saṃh. vol. i. p. 34.

2 These constant offerings have no expressly declared fruit, and therefore naturally look forward to some such transcendental fruit as that declared in the line from the Gítá.

3 This is part of the speech of King Vichaknu, on seeing oxen slaughtered at a great sacrifice.

4 See Aitareya Bráhmaṇa, ii. 11.

But the "water of his feet" means water for washing the feet, as otherwise it would not apply to all cases. (67).

a. The following passage occurs in Smṛiti (Nṛisiṃha Puráṇa, § 59),

"Those sacred waters of Ganges, Prayága, Gaya, Pushkara, and Naimisha, and those of Karujángala and Yamuná, only cleanse sinners after a lapse of time; but the water of Bhagavat's feet cleanses immediately."

Now does this "water of Bhagavat's feet" mean water actually connected with his feet, or water poured on the feet of his adopted representative (as an idol or priest)? The "water of his feet" means only "water for washing the feet" [*i.e.* we name it from its object, but we do not undertake to prove that it has actually been in contact with his feet]. Why? Because otherwise it would not apply to some cases which ought to be included. Thus we may at once declare that no direct connexion is possible between the water and Bhagavat; nor can it be by means of a personal descent of the deity, because this too cannot be [immediately] present to the performer of the ceremony. And again, even if we maintained that the difficulty was met by the actual connexion between the water and the feet of the consecrated image which receives the worship, still this would not hold in the case where an unconsecrated image is brought in for worship; nor again would it apply in the case of the Śálagrám Ammonites, etc., since these have no feet at all. So in order to help the passage to apply to all these cases, let the expression be held to mean only "water for washing the feet," as otherwise we should have to invent all kinds of very distant connexions which might be supposed to exist between the image, etc. [and the deity].

What is given by the worshipper himself may also be taken by him, since there is no difference. (68).

b. The offered eatables, the flowers left at an offering, etc., which were given in worship to Bhagavat, are to be given to the Sátwatas, as enjoined by the passage, "what is sacred to Vishṇu is for the Sátwatas,"[1] etc.; now as the word Sátwata applies equally to both, they may be also taken by the votary himself [as well as Kṛishṇa's other votaries], *i.e.* they may be appropriated to his own use by eating [as the food], or by holding [as the flowers]. If he himself takes them, the final ceremony[2] is fulfilled. But all trickery in religious rites is to be avoided. Therefore, just as the purodáśa cake, which was presented to Agni, etc., is afterwards given away, in the concluding ceremony, in accordance with the words of the injunction, "he cuts the offering to Agni Swishṭakṛit from the upper half; the four priests, with the institutor as the fifth, eat the cake,"—so here too the same thing is done because of the words of the injunction; otherwise one could not give it even to the Sátwatas, as it is property belonging to another.

If you rejoin that "he gives it to the Sátwatas from the injunction," I reply that there is nothing in the words of the injunction to exclude one's self. Nor may you retort, "But then you might argue in the same way that, when it is said 'let him give to the bráhmans,' he may give to himself as he too is a bráhman;"—because the very essence of giving is that while your own right of property in the thing is destroyed, another's right is constituted.[3] But we are not to apply this rule in the case of the concluding ceremony mentioned above, because we see that the institutor is expressly named in the injunction as a sharer; that is, the ceremony establishes his right, just as buying does. And so, if there are no other Sátwatas to benefit by the offerings, the rule is to be prevented from remaining inoperative, by himself taking them.

And the same principle is also to be understood when he

1 Sátwata originally means a prince of the Satwats, and is applied to Kṛishṇa; it afterwards means a devoted follower of Kṛishṇa.

2 Called *pratipatti* in the ritual treatises; *i.e.* the final disposal of what is left at the end of the rite, cf. Jaiminíya Nyáya M. V. iii. 4. 21.

3 I read परस्वत्वापादन° for परस्वत्वापादान° in p. 46, l. 3 *infra* (cf. last line), (cf. Jaiminíya Nyáya M. V. iv. 2. 12).

takes the water for washing the feet, etc., which he had himself presented. The line in the Gítá (iii. 12), "He is verily a thief, who eats things given by the gods, not having first given them to them," is to be explained as bearing out our view, for, as the agent is the same in the two clauses, so we must understand the object to be the same, as his supposed right of ownership is destroyed[1] [by the fact of the things having been previously given by him]; since the negation with the indeclinable participle [*apradáya*—'not having first given'] necessarily requires to be construed as applying to the same object as the verb 'he eats,'—as there is no reason for supposing that 'things given by the gods' could mean in the next clause things of a similar kind[2] [and not those very things]. Therefore we must hold that even what is presented to the gods may be used by the offerer if there is nothing to hinder it.

We must determine as to the different offences, by having regard to their occasion and character.[3] (69).

c. We find that [in the Varáha Puráṇa, § 124], in the passage beginning with the line, "Thirty-two offences in divine worship are enumerated," thirty-two offences and their several expiations are laid down. Now the question arises: is the avoidance of all offences a part of the worship, or is the avoidance of some of them a part of the worship and of some of them an end in itself? We find it said in reference to this point [Varáha P. *ib.*],

"Whatever man worships me with a flower improper for the rite, I will declare that man's fall [into hell]; hear it, O earth."

[1] स्वत्वध्वंसे seems irrelevant. My paṇḍit proposes त्वक्रान्तांशे.

[2] *i.e.* he quotes this verse of the Gítá as bearing out his own view, since he explains it as meaning that the offerer is to offer first, and then to use himself those very same things which he has offered. The two interpretations differ, inasmuch as one explains it 'not having first given *similar things* to the gods,' the other 'not having first given *them* to the gods.'

[3] In Aph. 69 read निमित्तगुणव्यपेक्षणात्. The ā in the printed text is a misprint, as the ă is the reading of Dr. Ballantyne's own MS. as well as that in the Sansk. Coll. Lib.

Here as improper flowers are positively forbidden, their avoidance can form no part of the worship. If, however, they are offered by a mistake in the course of the celebration of the ceremony, there is an expiation which has reference to that particular 'occasion.' But—[Varáha P. *ib.*] "When any one offers me incense, without having given me perfume and garlands,"—as here there is an offence committed against the proper order of the worship, and as this very order is a part of the worship, we must consider its expiation also as a part too, since we thereby avoid the worship's becoming defective; [and we thus have regard to the 'character' of the offence.] But when it is said [Varáha P. *ib.*] without any form of worship being mentioned, "But whoever approaches me, not having chewed a twig," etc., here it is clear that the avoidance of this offence is an end in itself as leading to happiness. Thus we determine the relative position of the different offences in regard to worship.—

[After this digression respecting these three incidental questions, he now returns to his main subject.]

It being thus established that worship is connected with faith, the passage (Gítá, ix. 26), "He who gives me with faith a leaf, flower, fruit, or water, I eat it from him pure-souled as offered with faith," declares that all gifts directed to Bhagavat are subordinate parts of faith. He proceeds to explain this in the next Aphorism;

The giving of a 'leaf,' etc., [in the Gítá is enjoined as a part of faith;][1] *otherwise the gift would be limited.* (70).

There is a well-known passage,

"Whatever is most desired in the world, whatever else is loved at home,—that is all to be given to the discus-holding god of gods, to please him."

Now the passage in the Gítá really enjoins that the gift of

[1] I supply as the rest of the sentence after *patráder dánam*, भक्त्यङ्गतया विधीयते.

everything to Bhagavat, already enjoined by this and other such passages, is a subordinate part of faith; otherwise, if the Gítá passage were the primary authority for giving, the gift would have to be limited to the four things especially named. If it be suggested that these four things may be definitely enjoined here [to supplement the general but vague injunction already given elsewhere],—we reply that in that case there ought to have been four separate sentences[1] [and not one, as at present]. Therefore the passage from the Gítá properly only re-enforces the gift already enjoined, and then itself enjoins that this gift is a subordinate part of faith, just as the Vedic passage [Taitt. Saṃh. ii. 5. 11], "he wears his cord over his left shoulder," which mode of wearing it is the general one [and already enjoined by the Smṛiti], has itself an enjoining force, inasmuch as it enjoins this mode of wearing it at that particular time as a subordinate part of the general whole, *i.e.* the great sacrifice at the new moon.[2]

[1] There is a favourite principle in the Púrva Mímâṃsâ, that several different characteristic circumstances cannot be enjoined in one sentence in regard to a thing which is already enjoined by a previous rule, as this would involve the fault called Vâkyabheda,—they must be broken up and mentioned separately. Thus when it is said (see p. 53, *suprà*), "let him who desires cattle sacrifice with the *chitrá*," the opponent suggests that *chitrá* is not here the name of a sacrifice, but means 'a spotted she-goat,' and thus only gives two special characteristics of sex and colour which the animal, already enjoined by other passages but unspecified, is to possess. This is rejected on the ground that, as the sacrifice is one already enjoined, these two qualities could not be combined in one word *chitrá*, but must have been given as separate sentences (see Nyâya Mâlâ V. i. 4. 3. cf. Taitt. Saṃh. Comm. ii. 4. 6).

[2] This also refers to several discussions of the Mímâṃsâ (see Taitt. Saṃh. Comm. vol. ii. p. 665, vol. i. p. 33). The injunction in question occurs in the 11th chapter in Taitt. Saṃh. ii. 5. Now the whole of the 5th section is devoted to the New-moon sacrifice; in the 7th and 8th ch. we have the *Sámidhení* hymns; in the 9th the *Nivid* sentences, and in the 10th some voluntary *Sámidhenís*. The Mímâṃsâ discussion shows that the injunction about the cord is not to be considered a part of the *sámidhenís* nor of the *nivids*, but of the general topic of the book, the New-moon sacrifice. The discussion in vol. i. p. 34, showed that the sentence "he wears his cord" is a definite injunction (*vidhi*), although it is expressed in the indicative, not the imperative mood; and though in itself it is *prápta*, (*i.e.* previously enjoined as the ordinary mode of wearing the cord (by the Smṛiti and Smârta-sútras) it is also an injunction, as it authoritatively declares that the act of so wearing it is here a part of the New-moon sacrifice.

These various forms of faith are the chief things, since they spring from previous good works, and are causes of the highest faith. (71).

These various forms of faith are the chief things in all ceremonial actions, because they tend to produce the highest faith, and because they are themselves produced by the other religious acts. Thus it is said (Gítá, iv. 10, 11),

"Many, being purified by knowledge and asceticism, have attained to faith in me;[1] and in what measure they turn to me, in that measure I show my favour to them."

Again, it is said elsewhere,

"Do not fishes dwell in the [holy] water of Ganges? The flocks of birds dwell in the home of the gods [the sky]. Being destitute of faith, they receive no benefit from a place of pilgrimage or the most sacred temple."

So, too,[2] in the line (Gítá, vii. 16),

"Four classes of men, all having done good works, worship
me with faith, Arjuna;"

as their respective degrees of faith thus spring from previous good works, faith in any of its degrees is superior to them [as being their fruit and end]. Hence we conclude that, as we said before, this whole discussion of ours belongs to a Mímáṃsá of Faith, not a Mímáṃsá of works.[3]

"But may we not say that those who have faith cannot be divided into a higher and lower class; because if they could be, how could Bhagavat speak of them as all standing on the same level, when he says (Gítá, vii. 16),

'Four classes of men, all having done good works, worship
me with faith, Arjuna;
He who is distressed, he who desires knowledge, he who
desires happiness, and he who knows, O hero.'"

[1] Swapneśwara expressly takes *madbhávam* as meaning here *madbhaktim*; but other commentators more rightly understand it as "have attained to identity with me."

[2] For तया in p. 48, last line, read तथा.

[3] Cf. Comm. on Aphorism 26.

The author replies in the following Aphorism,

The three are subordinate, and their association with the other is to give them honour. (72).

Three of these forms of faith are subordinate, and the Śruti's mentioning them in conjunction with the principal one is only to give honour to them by associating them with it, just as we see that ministers are mentioned together with the king. And thus the faith of 'the distressed' means the remembering (Kṛishṇa), repeating his names, etc., for the sake of destroying sin, deliverance from calamity, etc. The faith of 'him who desires knowledge' is the performance of sacrifices, etc., for the sake of knowledge. [This is one kind. But again] as it is said [in the Bṛihad Áraṇyaka,] "Him the Bráhmans desire to comprehend by studying the Veda, by sacrifice, charity, asceticism, and fasting," so we read [in the Gítá, xviii. 46],

"Having worshipped him by his own proper works, a man attains perfection;"

and again [in the Vishṇu Puráṇa, III. vii. 20],

"Him who never deviates from the duties of his caste,—who looks with equal mind on himself, or his friend, or his adversary,—who takes nothing from another, and smites none down,—him, fixed in mind, know to be Vishṇu's faithful worshipper."

We see by such passages that the faith called the desire of knowledge also consists in the performance for the sake of knowledge of the duties of one's own caste and order, the prescribed repetition of the Veda, etc. The faith which is called 'the desire of happiness' is also of two kinds,—the one before described which is carried out for the sake of the highest faith, and the other that which consists in repeating the divine names, etc., and is performed for the sake of sovereignty, heaven, etc. As it is said [in the Vishṇu Puráṇa, III. viii. 6],

"When Vishṇu is pleased, a man obtains all terrestrial enjoyments,—a supreme place and one to be praised even by the dwellers in heaven,[1]—yea, and even final liberation[2] which is best of all."

Here final liberation is attained by means of the highest faith, and therefore this form of faith, which we call 'a desire for happiness,' may have as its end this highest faith, since this exactly agrees with those words of the Gítá (ix. 19),

"Whosoever worship me with faith, they are in me, and I in them."

And as for what is said in the Bhágavata (VII. v. 22, 23),

"To hear and repeat the names of Vishṇu, to remember them, to serve his feet, to honour him, to shew him reverence, to do service as his slave, to love him as a friend, and to surrender oneself to him,—if this ninefold faith be yielded by a man to Vishṇu, [that I consider the best lesson,]"

these must be distributed according to circumstances among those divisions of ours. And there is no real fault in these artificial characteristics, even although the subject-matter of each should not be always kept distinct.

"But if repeating the divine names, and the like, were called [in Aph. 58] subordinate parts of faith, how can they now be considered as principal by being associated with the so-called faith of 'distress,' etc.?" To meet this, we have the next Aphorism.

Both may be included and also external, as the Aveshṭi and the Bṛihaspati-offering. (73).

Remembering and reciting the divine names, etc., inasmuch as they are subordinate parts of the highest faith, are included in it; but inasmuch as Śruti mentions another independent fruit arising from them, [beside the one arising from the highest faith], they may be separated from it and regarded as outside; just as in the Mímáṃsá discussions the expiatory

[1] The Commentary to the Vishṇu P. explains this as meaning the world of Brahmá, etc.

[2] *Nirváṇa* in the original.

ceremony called *aveshṭi*,[1] although included in the Rájasúya sacrifice, may still be regarded as a principal rite [and not ancillary], from its being connected with an independent fruit of its own, and so may be severed from that sacrifice. Or just as the Bṛihaspati offering, which is sometimes a principal rite, is properly ancillary to the Vájapeya sacrifice.[2] This distinction entirely depends on whether there is authority in the Śruti for it or not.[3]

So too it is said,

"If, when men are performing some rite, anything fails in the sacrifice, it will be supplied by remembering Vishṇu; thus saith the Śruti."

By this passage we see that all ceremonial rites can be occasionally performed as subordinate [to faith in Vishṇu, and dependent on it for their success, however they may in their ordinary relation occupy the principal place]. Thus there is nothing inconsistent in the supposition that these actions [reciting the divine names, etc.] may be in themselves subordinate parts of the highest faith and yet be principal in relation to the fruit of heaven which they will produce.

A particular distinction is now examined in 'the faith of distress.'

Remembering, reciting, hearing or telling the history, etc. [are included] in the 'faith of distress,' because they have the nature of expiation. (74).

Remembering and reciting the divine names, hearing or telling Bhagavat's history, acts of homage, etc., are properly included in the faith of the 'distressed,' since they are described as producing the cancelling of such and such sins to

[1] This ceremony is described in Taitt. Saṃh. I. viii. 19, and Sáyaṇa in his Comm. quotes the Mímáṃsá discussion. Cf. Jaiminíya Nyáya M. V. xi. 4. 3.

[2] This ceremony is to be performed by one who wishes to become a family priest, as Bṛihaspati was to the gods; it is described in the Taitt. Bráhmaṇa, II. vii. 1.

[3] The Sansk. Coll. MS. takes this line as a new Sútra and not as part of the Commentary, and reads प्रमाद्- for प्रमाण-, thus connecting it with what follows and not with what precedes.

those who are suffering the pain of hell caused by those sins. Thus we read [in the Vishṇu Puráṇa, II. vi. 32, 33],

"Arduous expiations for great sins, trifling ones for minor offences, have been propounded, O Maitreya, by Swáyambhuva and others. But whatever be the expiatory acts, whether penances, deeds of charity, or the like,—to remember Kṛishṇa is superior to them all;"

Again [ibid. VI. vii.],

"That repetition of his name with faith, Maitreya, which is the best consumer of all sins, as fire is of metals."

So too [Mahábh. xii. § 345],

"To visit all hermitages, to bathe in all places of pilgrimage, confers not such blessings, O Sauti, as the history of Náráyaṇa. Men become purified in body, when they have heard this holy history from the beginning,—whose subject is Náráyaṇa, and which abolishes all sin," etc.

Therefore it is quite proper that these should be included under the so-called faith of 'distress.'

If you object that the more difficult expiations will not be practised, we reply that from their including a period only ending in death,[1] *the lesser expiations [such as repetition of the divine names, etc.] must be ranked among the great expiations.* (75).

An objector may here say, "All this may be true, but it is clear, from the opposite being contrary to reason, that all these passages only refer to very small sins; otherwise all those penances which involve considerable pain would have so far lost their authoritativeness that no one would practise them." To this however we demur; since these supposed minor expiations really involve more pain, because they are described as including a period only ending at death.

Thus we read (Vishṇu Pur. II. vi. 29),

"Therefore, O sage, the man who remembers Vishṇu day and

[1] I would read आप्रायणं for आप्रयाणं.

night, being purified and having all his sins abolished, never goes to hell."

Such a passage means that this habit is to continue as long as life continues, and end only with that; since the beginning and the end agree [in being undefined and therefore contemporary with life]. For no time is specified for the beginning; if it had been, we might have been led to suppose, from the contradiction to this, that the end also could have a different meaning [from that which is its obvious one, and imply a fixed time too]. And thus, as both kinds of expiation are alike in the amount of pain which they involve, we need not suppose that the other kinds of penance will become, as our objector fears, unauthoritative and cease to be practised. The passage (in the Vishṇu Pur. II. vi. 35),

> "At morning and night, sunset and noon, remembering Vishṇu,"

which divides the worship into different fixed periods [and so might seem to contradict our view], is really only a repetition (*anuváda*).

Nor is this expiation which we are advocating only suited for one who is repenting for some act of sin. As for the passage (in the Vishṇu P. *ibid.*),

> "Whosoever having committed sin, feels repentance, his best expiation is one remembrance of Hari;"

since this is a reiteration (*anuváda*) of the necessity of repentance as a part of every expiation, the word 'one' must also be a reiteration of that comparative disregard of all other expiations which the whole argument of the previous passage had already established. Otherwise the two parts of the sentence would have to be divided and the objects of each would be special and not the same.[1] Therefore also the passages pre-

[1] *i.e.* the first part clearly declares what had been already enjoined (*i.e.* that repentance is necessary in every expiation), and it is therefore an *anuváda*; and the second part must also be an *anuváda*, unless we are to suppose that the two parts of the sentence (although connected by *yat* and *tat*) are different, the one being an *anuváda* or simple reiteration and the other an *arthaváda*.

viously quoted [sc. Vishṇu Pur. II. vi. 33, etc.] will similarly not be *arthavádas* but *anuvádas*,[1] as they also are severally involved in the same construction of the relative and its corresponding demonstrative [which unite the two clauses indissolubly].

Hence we read elsewhere [Vishṇu Pur. III. vii. 34, 35],

"Yama's attendants, their staves and bonds, Yama himself and his tortures, are powerless against him whose soul is always dependent on Keśava. Let him at all times and in all places repeat the names of the discus-armed one; no impurity is found in him, for He is the purifier."

This and other similar passages declare that the remembrance of Vishṇu should be continual.

[This, however, is not the whole truth, as the next Aphorism will declare.]

Even a little act in the case of the faithful worshipper destroys great sins, because of the abandonment of everything else. (76.)

'Even a little act,' as once remembering or repeating Bhagavat's name, etc., 'will destroy,' *i.e.* obliterate, 'great sins,' since in the case of the faithful worshipper there is the full idea of 'abandonment,' *i.e.* of giving up all other modes of expiation. As it is said in the Gítá (xviii. 66),

"Abandoning all religious acts, fly to me as thy one refuge; I will deliver thee from all sins, sorrow not."

[1] The *arthaváda* is properly a persuasive enforcement of a previous injunction; it gives the purpose of the injunction, and illustrates its power by positive or negative examples. Thus there is an *arthaváda* for the *Sarvajit* sacrifice (Táṇḍya Br. xvi. 7. 2), "Verily by the *sarvajit* the gods conquered all, it is for the attainment of all, for the conquest of all; by this a man attains all, conquers all." The *anuváda* is the reiteration or re-inculcation of an injunction, it may be with further details, but without dwelling on the purpose of the injunction itself. Thus, after the injunction 'he is to offer the *agnihotra*,' we have an *anuváda* 'he offers it with curds' (this is a *guṇánuváda*); or, again, we have an injunction 'let him who desires prosperity offer a white goat to Váyu,' followed by the *anuváda* 'the wind (Váyu) is the swiftest of gods' (Taitt. Saṃh. iii. 4. 3), this is a *stutyarthánuváda*. Later writers (as Laugákshi, etc.) make the *anuváda* one of the three kinds of *arthaváda*. This later view has probably produced a var. lect. in the Sansk. Coll. MS., which reads in p. 53, l. 1, *anuvádárthavádatwam* for *anuvádatwán-nárthavádatwam*.

Here the meaning cannot be that the sin spoken of is the previous abandonment of all 'voluntary' religious acts; for there is no sin in abandoning such religious acts [as they need not be performed unless by some one who desires the result which they are to produce], and so what sin would there be from which Bhagavat was to deliver his votary? "Well,—but suppose that it is other kinds of sin [arising from the neglect of positive duty] which are to be destroyed,—as it might well happen that the desire to escape the acquisition of merit [and the consequent necessity of future births in order to enjoy its reward] might have caused him to abandon voluntary religious acts." Still we cannot allow that the passage refers to the sin arising from the previous abandonment of 'necessary' or of 'occasional' religious acts,—because, if there is a positive and authoritative command for their abandonment, no sin will accrue from the act, what then will be the need of deliverance? And if you say that there is no such command, we demur, as the very text quoted from the Gítá contains such an injunction, and consequently the act commanded will not produce sin. If you reply that "the words 'having abandoned all religious acts' are clearly meant as a description by *anuváda* of the sannyásin [who has already done so by his profession, and not from this injunction], and therefore the passage refers to him"—I answer, No,[1] for the smṛiti lays down certain expiations for sannyásins, as that in the case of unchastity, etc.,[2] and your interpretation would give them an option [between these and faith], and your old fear would thus be actually realised [see suprà, Aph. 75,] that the practice of severe acts of asceticism would be given up. Nor can you allege that in the case of sannyásins these sins must be abolished by continual repetition of the deity's names [which was shown above to be equal to any single act of penance, however heavy,]—for we see by such lines as the following:

[1] न is often omitted after a púrvapaksha as here, cf. Muir, Sansk. Texts, iii. p. 61.
[2] See some of the expiations for an *avakírṇin* in Gautama's Institutes, xxiii. 17. xxv., but the sannyásin is not mentioned there.

"Even though filled with a great sin, if he meditates on Vishṇu for the twinkling of an eye,
The ascetic becomes again the purifier even of those who purify the company in which they dwell,"

that [in his case also] 'a little act' destroys great sins. And besides we have no right to introduce the idea of the *sannyásin* into the aphorism, as there is no mention in the context of that order of life (*áśrama*). Therefore just as in ordinary life, if any one were to promise to another, saying, "leaving all others, follow me and I will put an end to thy troubles," we should naturally understand that this implied the abandoning of all other means to abolish those troubles,—so too here the words of Bhagavat imply a similar abandonment of all other means to abolish sin. And if we read the whole chapter in its connexion with this one verse, even if this latter does seem to a certain degree to enjoin the sannyásin's mode of life, we shall see that such cannot be its real object, as the general subject and the context are of greater importance in determining the sense of a passage.[1] And in this very chapter such lines as that (śl. 2),

"By *sannyása* the seers understand the abandonment of all voluntary religious acts,"

distinctly speak of an abandonment of voluntary religious acts, not of the sannyásin order; and thus he alone who has resolved to abandon all other modes of expiation and desires to escape from his distress by repeating the names of Bhagavat only, can lay claim to the promises attached even to the single mention of his name. Nor can these various objections be simultaneously alleged against our view, for they really relate to different persons, [and therefore do not lend each other any mutual support].

Nor are the more difficult expiations here left unperformed through any fear of the trouble which they would involve; for such passages as (Gítá, xviii. 8),

"Whatever religious act he leaves unperformed through

[1] Cf. note on Aph. 15.

fear of bodily trouble, saying 'it is a pain to me,' that abandonment only springs from the principle of passion, and he will not gain the fruit of true abandonment,"
clearly teach that such abandonment as this is to be avoided.

And such passages as that in the Vishṇu Puráṇa [VI. viii. 21],

"The very terrible sin of men in the Kali age which gives them the pain of hell, is at once abolished by his name being once repeated," etc.,
distinctly refer to the privileges [of the faithful man].

So too such passages as that in the Gítá (ix. 30, 31),

"Even if a man of very wicked life worships me with undivided worship, he is to be esteemed virtuous, for he has resolved aright. Speedily does he become holy, he attains eternal rest; be assured, O son of Kuntí, my votary never perishes;"

And again that in the Nrisiṃha-puráṇa (viii. 28. 29),

"The inhabitants of hell [in their agony] cried out 'O Kṛishṇa,' 'O Kṛishṇa,' 'O Nárasiṃha;' thus was Vishṇu mentioned with faith by those in hell, and all the infernal pains of those great-souled ones were destroyed,"
clearly declare the privileges of faith. Here 'recitation' merely means the bare mention of the name, and there is no binding rule that it must be in the vocative case.

There is no need of the adjuncts of other expiations, because it stands in their place, like the post of the threshing-floor. (77).

When it is said in the Vishṇu-puráṇa (II. vi. 34),

"But his best expiation is one remembrance of Hari,"
the direct mention of the name [expiation] does not imply the need of the usual adjuncts of other expiations,—'because it stands in their place,' *i.e.* because it is enjoined in the place of all other expiations. Just as, when it is said (in Áśwaláyana's Śrauta-sútras, ix. 7), "the post of the threshing-floor is the sacrificial post," the rule enjoins that the post of

the threshing-floor is to be used for the sacrificial post in tying up the victim, but it does not follow that the substituted post must have eight corners,[1] etc., which characterise the true sacrificial post,—so here there is no need of such usual adjuncts of other expiations as cutting the nails, hair, etc.

But we must not say on the other hand that the recitation of Kṛishṇa's names is the only true expiation (*práyaśchitta*)[2] because it abolishes sin; for we see by the couplet [of Angiras' Smṛiti],

"'Penance' is called *práyas, chitta* means 'certainty;' *Práyaśchitta* it is therefore called in tradition as combined with penance and certainty,"[3]

that the word *práyaśchitta* primarily applies to some form of penance and is only secondarily used of other things [as, for instance, of the recitation in question].

Since the right to appropriate the subsidiary means[4] is determined by the right to appropriate the principal end [faith] which they serve,—we have next to examine who has the right to practise the faith which we have been discussing.

All, down even to the despised castes, are capable of learning it at second-hand, like the great common truths. (78).

'All are capable' of practising faith, 'down even to the despised castes,' such as Cháṇḍálas, etc.,—because there is no distinction in the universal desire to lay aside the misery of mundane existence. If any one objects, "how can this right belong to others than the three twice-born castes, since they have no right to read the Veda?" our author answers 'at second-hand.' Following the principle laid down in the Mímáṃsá Sútras (i. 1. 2), 'Duty is a thing recognised by the instigatory character (of the passage of Śruti which mentions

1 Cf. Taitt. Saṃhitá, vol. i. p. 487.

2 In p. 55, last line, read *práyaśchittatwam* with the Sanskrit Coll. MS.

3 We must read *tapo-niśchaya-saṃyuktam* in the second line. The śloka is quoted in the S'abda-kalpa-druma.

4 Sc. the inferior forms of faith (as repeating the divine names, etc.), see Aph. 58.

it),' and also that in the Vedánta Sútras (i. 1. 3), '(God's existence is known) from the Śástra being the source of our knowledge,'—we do not dispute that transcendental things can only be learned directly from Śruti. But knowledge based upon the Śruti may be still indirectly produced in women, Śudras, and others, by means of legends, puráṇas,[1] etc., and in Cháṇḍálas, etc., by such mediate teaching as is in accordance with the Smṛiti and immemorial good custom, just as they learn the great common truths of not injuring living beings, etc. Otherwise it would follow that even a knowledge of these latter would not be found in them.

Hence even those who have not attained perfection [are capable of it] in His world. (79).

Since all men alike are capable of it, those in whom the highest faith has not attained perfection in this world, are said in the Smṛiti to practise the various means to attain it in Śwetadwípa, the world of Bhagavat. Thus we read how they there practise the means to attain the highest faith [in the Mahábhárata, Śántiparvan, cccxxxviii. 12778–12792], in the passage commencing,

"To the north of the ocean of milk lies the splendid Śwetadwípa; there live men bright as the moon, intent on Náráyaṇa, filled with the idea of absolute Unity,—these are devoted to Purushottama," and ending,

"Then those men quickly ran up together, folding their hands full of joy and uttering shouts of praise; then I heard a great shout as they spoke,[2]—lo! an offering is presented by them to that deity."

Therefore all have a right to this doctrine of faith; and hence it has been said in the Vedánta Sútras (I. iii. 26), "Báda-

[1] This refers to the well-known passage of Smṛiti so often quoted by Hindu mediæval commentators, "the three Vedas are not to be heard by women, S'udras, and merely nominal Bráhmans,—therefore the Bhárata story was made by the sage (Vyása) through pity."

[2] हि वदतां Bombay ed. for विवदतां.

ráyaṇa [allows a right to study Vedánta doctrines] even to beings above man, since they too may need them."

He now introduces, as a digression, the question, "how is it that Bhagavat's world is not for those who have attained perfection?"

But [the afore-mentioned one is the true interpretation], as in this way the single stage and the successive stages are accounted for. (80).

The "but" is added to meet the doubt which has been suggested. The Náráyaṇíya section of the Śánti Parvan of the Mahábhárata (xii. § 346), after beginning with the line "Those who are exceedingly sinless in the world, delivered from merit and demerit," goes on to describe their successive entrance, by the door of the solar orb, into the bodies of Aniruddha, Pradyumna, and Saṃkarshaṇa;[1] and then it declares, "But those who have their minds intently fixed in contemplation, who are self-restrained, and sense-subdued, filled with the idea of absolute Unity, enter the son of Vasudeva."

Such is the description of the successive stages; but it is said afterwards (ibid. § 350),

"But they, whose every acquired desert has been already consumed as fuel in the world, and who are delivered from all merit or demerit—their destination has been thus declared by thee, as they pass by these intermediate stages; and in this fourth stage they arrive at the highest sphere. But verily this doctrine of absolute Unity is the best of all and dear to Nárá-

1 "Those who are exceedingly sinless in the world, delivered from merit and demerit,—to them as they go on their happy journey, O best of the twice-born, the sun who dispels darkness in all the world is declared the door; their bodies being consumed by the sun, being invisible by any one anywhere, having become atomic, they verily enter that deity; released from him, they then enter into the body of Aniruddha, and having become pure mind they enter into Pradyumna, and released from Pradyumna they enter the living Saṃkarshaṇa, they the best of the twice-born, Sánkhyas and Bhágavatas. Then being freed from the three *guṇas*, they quickly enter into the Supreme Spirit, the unconditioned Soul. Know thou that the son of Vasudeva is verily the Soul, the abode of all." Then follows the couplet quoted in the text, "but those who have their minds, etc."

yaṇa, whereby they attain to the immortal Hari, without passing by the three preliminary stages."

Here we have the doctrine of one stage only declared as the end of those who possess perfect faith. Otherwise, [but for this distinction between perfect and imperfect faith,] there would be a manifest contradiction between the two accounts. Therefore we conclude that the attainment of Bhagavat's world (Śweta-dwípa) belongs to those whose faith is imperfect.

And from the remainder of the passage in the Smṛiti[1] *relating to the soul's departure.* (81).

There is a passage in the Gítá, relating to the soul's departure at death, beginning, "endowed with faith and strength of devotion" (viii. 10), which says (viii. 13), "he who goes forth and abandons the body, pronouncing the syllable Om which is Brahman, and remembering me, he goes the highest way." The remainder of the passage follows (in śl. 24) and declares the successive stages of the way by which the soul is to go,

"The fire, the light, the day, the waxing moon, the six months of the sun's northern journey,—those who go forth by these, reach Brahman, as men who know Bṛahman."

So also in the remainder of the immediate context (as given in śl. 16),

"All worlds, Arjuna, up to the heaven of Brahman, admit of a return; but when a man reaches me, O son of Kuntí, there is for him no other birth."

Here by the mention at first of the different worlds, and then by the force of the preposition *upa* in *mám upetya*, "when a man reaches me," it is clearly implied that the attainment of the worlds near to Bhagavat is only for those whose faith is imperfect; but for him whose faith is perfect even such a reward as going to His world is not suited, because *his* reward is of course imperishable, and we hear in Śruti that in *his* world they do not practise the means [for increasing faith, as

[1] The Sansk. Coll. MS. omits the word *smṛiti* in the Aphorism.

it is already perfect[1]]. And again, if it were established that imperfect faith could from that world certainly secure a gradual liberation, the injunction to remember Bhagavat's name at the moment of death would be needless. Nor can we say that by dwelling in Bhagavat's world the highest faith is superadded to the other; for we are taught clearly by that line of the Gítá (viii. 22),

> "This supreme Soul, O son of Pṛithá, is to be attained by undeviating faith,"

that this faith is the means of liberation, independently of any other. Therefore all that we can concede is that even in the world of Bhagavat [as elsewhere] a soul has the power of attaining this highest faith. But birth in the favoured land of Bháratavarsha is only useful as being the indispensable condition for performing meritorious ceremonial works, as it is said in the Vishṇu Puráṇa (II. iii. 5),

> "No where else are ceremonial acts enjoined to mortals."

But we have shown before that faith is not a ceremonial work [and is therefore independent of country]. If you rejoin that [by being born elsewhere] a man would still fail to obtain its indispensable conditions,—we answer that if the main end is allowed to be attainable, the necessary conditions and adjuncts are thereby included, just like the adjunct [fire] of the sacrifice of a Nisháda king.[2] And again, Śúdras, etc., are prohibited from ceremonies which arise out of Vedic hymns, but not from the appointed means of producing faith, such as re-

[1] While these means are practised in S'wetadwípa, etc., cf. Comm. on Aphorism 79.

[2] This refers to a Vedic passage quoted in Kátyayána's S'rauta-sútras, i. 1. 12, "He whose subjects Rudra destroys, should offer a *charu*-oblation of *Coix barbata*; let the priest cause the Nisháda king to offer this sacrifice." The question is discussed in S'abara's Mímáṃsá-bháshya (vi. 8. 20, 21), whether this offering should be made in a consecrated fire duly laid or in common fire. He decides that it should be in a common fire,—as fire is the adjunct of a ceremonial work, but the ceremony of duly laying it (*ádhána*) is only an adjunct of fire, and though fire by an express Vedic injunction is a *necessary* adjunct of a ceremonial work, it is not so with the *ádhána* ceremony, unless, as in the Dars'apúrṇamása, it is expressly mentioned by the śruti, which is not the case in the present sacrifice.

membering and repeating Bhagavat's name, etc. Since then it is clearly established that all classes have a right to practise faith, all idea that knowledge is an indispensable preliminary is improper.

"Well then, let it be granted that even those who have committed great sins are competent to attain the highest faith, —they will be similarly competent for the ancillary parts of knowledge, which is itself an ancillary part of faith,—these ancillary parts being the repetition of the text of the Veda, etc." He replies,

But the great sinners [are competent only] for the faith of distress. (82).

But those who have been devoted to sins which will lead to the soul's falling into a lower state [as hell or an animal birth], are competent for the faith of distress only, just as they require expiations [cf. Aph. 74], and not for the other forms of faith; since the abolition of those sins is more requisite for them than anything else, in accordance with such passages as this, 'enjoying he would increase his sin,' etc. When the sin is abolished, of course their competence for the highest faith is more firmly established than ever.

As the question naturally suggests itself from the consideration of the perfect soul, devoted to the Supreme, he next proceeds to dispel the demon-like doubt whether all religious duties are different from the highest faith or not.

This [highest faith] is the true identity with the Supreme, since this is recognised as the meaning of the Gítá. (83).

This highest faith is the true identity with the Supreme, and nothing else [*i.e.* the summum bonum of the soul;] since we hear in the Śruti[1] that this is distinctly recognised as the meaning of the Gítá. Thus we read in the Náráyaṇíya section

[1] If *śravaṇa* is used correctly here, it would seem to imply that the term S'ruti can be applied to the Mahábhárata itself, and not merely to the Gítá included in it.

of the Śánti book of the Mahábhárata [§ 350], that Janamejaya asks,

"Those bráhmans who, duly intent and practising all the injunctions, read the Vedas with the Upanishads, and those who follow the duties of the ascetics,—I know of a way better than theirs, the way of the absorbed monotheists;[1] by what god or ṛishi has this religion been taught?"

Vaiśampáyana answers,

"When the troops of the Kuru and Páṇḍava hosts met in battle array, when Arjuna was full of despondency, this was sung by Bhagavat himself." Therefore the highest faith [as described in the Gítá] is identification with the Supreme.

"Still even the inferior forms may directly produce liberation,—what harm will it do, if you concede this?" He replies,

Only by producing the highest faith do all [lead to liberation]; thus verily He saith. (84).

Only by producing the highest faith, do all [religious duties] become means to liberation. Thus verily saith Bhagavat, adding at the same time the reason (Gítá, xviii. 68),

"Whosoever shall declare this most excellent mystery to my faithful votaries, he, having produced the highest faith in me, shall without doubt come to me."

Now since it had been already established that the fruit of the teaching of this doctrine was the becoming identified with Brahman, why is it here added "having produced the highest faith in me"? Because the śruti declares that *this* is the means to liberation. Therefore in the legend of the king Uparichara Vasu, when it is said (Mahábhárata, xii. § 337), "His kingdom, his wealth, his wife and his chariot,—he always consecrated them, saying, 'it all belongs to Bhagavat';" this is given as a distinguishing sign of his faith, *i.e.* his intense affection for the Supreme Lord,—since it could not have been done simply for itself [but must have been a means to some

[1] *Ekántin.*

higher end]. Therefore, when the Śruti speaks of all religious duties as causes of liberation, we infer that it really means that they are helpful to produce liberation, inasmuch as they produce the highest form of faith. It is not possible that a religious duty could produce both [*i.e.* this faith and liberation too], because, being an action, it could not produce [such a transcendental end as] liberation; and therefore the injunction to perform it must have reference to a visible effect [*i.e.* to one which arises in this present life, as the production of faith in the soul].

Thus ends the second daily portion of the second chapter of the Commentary on the hundred Aphorisms of Śáṇḍilya, composed by the most learned teacher Swapneśwara.

THIRD CHAPTER.

Since the pre-eminence of faith arises from the pre-eminence of its object, and also because of the promised identity of the faithful worshipper with Him, He, the object of faith's adoration, is now described.

The object of worship[1] *is this Being without a second, since all is identical with Him.* (85).

The certainty [*i.e.* the real existence] of the object depends on knowledge,—such is the conclusion of the Śástras; existence is knowledge.[2] But existence is not a genus, because genus does not exist in genus, etc.,[3] nor even if it were would the desired connexion be established, from the cumbrousness of the process. Therefore the one existence, the supreme Brahman, who by himself pervades all things, is himself knowledge. In all visible things there is really identity with Him; even [the

1 The two Sansk. Coll. MSS. read *bhajaníyam* for *bhajaníyena.*

2 The commentary on the third chapter is mostly in verse; hence it is very elliptical and obscure. I have been obliged to supplement the text by copious notes, for which I gratefully acknowledge the assistance which I have received from Paṇḍit Maheśa Chandra Nyáyaratna.

3 The Vedánta doctrine is that nothing exists but Brahman, and He is pure intelligence; nothing else exists except so far as it is known as identical with Him. The Nyáya, however, maintains that Existence is a summum genus, 'as no genus except Existence, belongs to each and to all of the three categories of Substance, Quality, and Action' [Ballantyne, Siddh. Muktáv. p. 20]; it denies that there can be a genus of the three Categories, Genus, Difference, or Intimate Relation [cf. *Ibid.* p. 19], and holds that these Categories (with Non-existence) are not genera or classes (*játi*), but general characteristics (*upádhi*). Our author maintains that existence is not a genus, and tries to establish it by a quibble,—'because of the non-existence of genus in genus' [sc. if genus had a genus, then that genus would have its genus, and so on *ad infinitum*]. The opponent answers "I quite grant that genus cannot exist in genus by intimate relation; but suppose that it exists in it by the relation of identity." Our author replies,—even so it would not help your view; you do not want this relation of identity which leads to no result, you really want the connexion to be that of intimate relation, which properly connects the genus or species with the classes or individuals in which it resides, and it is *this* to which we stoutly demur.

apparent] diversity is found only in what depends on the real.[1] If you reply that, if this were true, we should conceive of a jar as 'knowledge,' just as we conceive that 'a jar is,'—I reply that we do not thus conceive of a jar, viz. that it *is*, since it does not present itself to our senses in any other than a transitory connexion.[2] [Again, the Naiyáyik objector supposes that] the causes of creation[3] are (i) God's knowledge, embracing as its proper object the material cause which he has to act upon; (ii) his desire to create; and (iii) his consequent effort of will; but if these three causes have to be assumed, together with the object on which they are to work, our supposition of one only cause is far more simple. This one Brahman whom we postulate as our cause, together with His object to work on, [viz. the material cause, Ignorance], is not a substratum of qualities,[4] because this is a cumbrous hypothesis; the supposition, that he is a knower, etc., only arises, as in the parallel case of time,[5] through the disguising influence of a limitation imposed *ab extra* [*i.e.* it is our understanding, acting as a disguiser, which divides the one ever-flowing stream of time into

[1] This is the only sense which I can give for the line as read in the printed text: तदभेदो दृश्यमात्रे दृश्यभेदस्तु सत्परे। The Sansk. Coll. MSS. read दृश्यते वस्तुसत्परे, which may perhaps mean, "identity with Him is seen in all visible things, as soon as they are viewed as depending entirely on the one only existing thing."

[2] We see it only as *γιγνόμενον*, not *ὄν*. The Paṇḍit explained it *ghaṭasya bháne 'pi na tatra sattárúpa-satyatwena ghaṭasya bhánaṃ, tad-rúpeṇa ghaṭasya anupasthiteḥ, paraṃtu vidyamánatwa-rúpa-sattayá.* The jar *really* only exists in Brahman and is therefore knowledge; but this relates to its transcendental state, not to its phenomenal state.

[3] The two Sansk. Coll. MSS. and the Oxford MS. read *vishaya-jnána* for *vishaye jnána-* in p. 62, l. 2; and I have conjectured *hetutá* for *hetuná* (though all the MSS. read the latter), as it offers a clearer sense. If we read *hetuná*, it must be taken in connexion with the *hetutwe* of line 3, and we have the same meaning, but more obscurely expressed.

[4] He is not the possessor of knowledge, a desire to create, and will, as the Nyâya would maintain; he is himself pure knowledge. Cf. Zanche, *de nat. Dei*, "Hæc est causa cur verius appelletur Deus vita quam vivens, sapientia quam sapiens, lux quam lucidus, atque ita de reliquis. Quamobrem? Quia seipso vivit, non per vitam; se ipso perque suam essentiam sapiens est, non per sapientiam aliquam quæ essentiæ divinæ sit addita;" Cyprian, ep. 52, "Unus ille et verus Pater, bonus, misericors, et pius; immo ipsa bonitas, misericordia, et pietas."

[5] In p. 62, l. 5, I read (with Sansk. Coll. MS.) *kálasyevopádhi-* for *kálavedyopádhi-*.

definite portions, as minutes, days, months, years, etc.; and similarly our imperfection conditions God as knowing, wishing, and willing].

His Máyá-power (is known) from the totality of the non-intelligent creation. (86).

'His,' *i.e.* Brahman's, almighty power is Máyá (or Illusion), —as is declared in the Gítá (vii. 14),

"Verily this my Máyá-power, consisting of the three qualities, is hard to be overpassed; they only who come to me (with faith) cross over this Máyá;"

And again, (ix. 10),

"Through me as its superintendent nature brings forth the universe; for this reason, O son of Kuntí, the world revolves in its round of change."

But this Divine power is called Máyá,[1] from the marvellousness of its effects, not from their unreality, since Śruti declares the existence of Bráhman expressly to prove the existence of his effect, the world;[2] and to assume the falseness of the latter would be improper, as it would involve the non-reality of its cause. If you reply that "the characteristic mark of falseness is its being abolished by the knowledge of reality," we still demur, for if, as you Vedántists hold, the world's very falseness is itself false, its truth [or reality] is only more firmly established;[3] and if, on the other hand, you hold that its [inferred] falseness is *true*, the truth of what is presented by our senses seems to be established [since perception is a superior test to inference]. And again, since things which are utterly unreal cannot be illumined, the very fact that the inanimate world has to be illumined by

[1] Our author takes *máyá* in its old sense of 'ausserordentliches Vermögen, Wunderkraft,' as it is used in the Rigveda, see the St. Petersb. Dict. *sub v.*

[2] As in the Chhándogya Upanishad, "Verily in the beginning this was existent, one only, without a second" (vi. 1), and "He whose will is truth" (iii. 14).

[3] One of the cardinal tenets of the Vedánta is that the ignorance which causes the world, is itself false as being imagined by ignorance; but if so, the falsity of a falsity is *truth*, as *minus* into *minus* gives *plus*.

soul,[1] proves that it is true; for the supposed manifestation of a non-existing snake in a rope is really only a case of mistake,[2] [not a creation of ignorance]; for it is an acknowledged rule in all other things except undeveloped Nature, [*i.e.* in all creation,[3]] that their reality or unreality depends on their being capable or not of being contradicted [or falsified] by a more authoritative judgment.[4] This Máyá is the totality of the non-intelligent creation, and as it is capable of being known, it must be real, otherwise a universal rule would be at once contradicted;[5] therefore Brahman, the pure Intelligence, and the unintelligent Creation are both real.[6]

And from the identity of the special categories with [their material causes] the general. (87).

Thus, too, we see that the special categories[7] arise from the general, and the general are held to be the material causes of the special because they are identical with them [as the cause

[1] Cf. Vedánta-sára, p. 16, "all the inanimate world (*i.e.* the non-Soul) from the 'son' up to the 'void,' has to be illumined by Intelligence (*i.e.* Soul)."

[2] *Anyatháḱhyáti* 'mistake' is the Naiyáyik explanation,—the mistaken spectator erroneously transfers the idea of the snake which he had actually seen elsewhere, to the rope now before him; the Vedántin, on the other hand, holds that a snake is then and there actually produced,—only as it belongs to the class of 'apparent' things (*prátibhásika*) and not 'practical' (*vyávahárika*), we get rid of it by applying to it that contradiction which the world of practical life supplies. The two views are beautifully contrasted in the Vedánta-paribhásha, p. 10, ll. 13-16.

[3] Prakṛiti being imperceptible and therefore not capable of being thus falsified (*bádha*).

[4] Jars, houses, etc., really exist, because no superior evidence 'falsifies' them and precludes their reality; but the objects seen in dreams, the snake seen in a rope, etc., are falsified and precluded by waking sight or by closer inspection. I follow the readings here of the two Sansk. Coll. MSS.

अन्यत्र सदसत्त्वाभ्यां बाधाबाधव्यवस्थितेः ।
सा माया जडसामान्यं ज्ञेयं तु नित्यमेव तत् ॥
अन्यथा त्वव्यवस्था स्यात् तस्माच्चिज्जाड्यनित्यता ।

[5] *i.e.* that if a thing is capable of being known, it must exist; we cannot know the non-existent.

[6] I take *nitya* as here meaning *sat*.

[7] See my note, *suprà*, on Aph. 48.

is always identical with its effect.[1] So too, in the same way, Brahman is identical with the world, as its material cause, —it exists by his existence.] It will not do to hold [with the follower of the Nyáya] that the connexion between the cause and its effect may be that called 'Intimate relation,' and not that called 'Identity,'—because it is a much more cumbrous assumption than ours and involves the connexion of 'difference';[2] and by our own we easily get at the true meaning of the various Śruti passages,—seizing them one by one, as oxen by their horns.[3] Hence the Supreme Lord's causality consists in his being in all his effects [as identical with them]; his efficiency arises from his knowledge extending to all objects which are to be known.[4] [Nor may our opponent assert with the Sánkhyas, that then mind (*buddhi*) might be the world's material cause,—for] even if mind were to be directly illumined by the Witness [Soul], still, since mind is properly itself unknowable, we should contradict, by our assumption that it could be known, the very definition of mind and extend it to cases where it cannot apply.[5]

[1] This is a favourite doctrine of Sanskrit philosophy, especially of the Sánkhya, from whence it was probably borrowed by the Vedánta. The bracelets, earrings, etc., made out of gold, are only gold after all.

[2] For two things to be related by Intimate relation, they must be originally different, i.e. *two* things; our assumption of their real identity is more simple and therefore better suits the Law of Parcimony.

[3] *i.e.* such passages as 'Uktha is Brahman,' 'Práṇa (breath) is Brahman,' etc. *S'ṛingagráhiká-nyáya* is a proverb sometimes explained as 'catching an unruly bull first by securing one horn and then the second,' and sometimes, 'driving many oxen into a stall, by seizing them one by one by their horns.' *Samayaḥ* in l. 5 seems to mean the same as *samanvayaḥ*.

[4] By the first he is their material cause, as the gold of the earrings; by the latter their efficient cause, as the goldsmith, since 'what a man knows, that he can do.'

[5] The Paṇḍit's note, which I translate, clears up most of the difficulty of this hard passage. "'But if *buddhi* is thus connected with all its objects, then why should not *buddhi* be the world's material cause, and not Íśwara?' He replies, 'if mind (*buddhi*), etc.' The meaning of the passage is as follows: The knowledge of visible objects, as jars, etc., is twofold, (*a*) the connection of the senses with the object [see note *infrà*, p. 100], and (*b*) the result obtained. By the former the concealing veil of ignorance is destroyed; by the second, which is the manifestation of intelligence or soul, as reflected on the mind which is evolved in connection with the object, we obtain the knowledge of the jar. (Or as it has been said, in more exact conformity to the Vedánta doctrine, 'the evolution (*vṛitti*) of the mind as associated with the object and the manifestation of

When Íśwara awakes from sleep,[1] after a mundane destruction, his intellect (*buddhi*) is the first thing that arises; and having contemplated thereby the various relations of causes, effects, etc., he, the Lord, proceeds to create the world. Although in itself without an object, yet as the disguising associate of His Intelligence, it abides as the oil in the lamp, etc., and illumines, revealing a specific character. Next from the volition 'I will make' arises the principle of Egoism, as is established by various passages of Śruti and Smṛiti, as, for instance, "He looked,—he thought, 'may I be multiplied.'"[2]

Since Egoism extends through all the developments of intellect, as wish, etc., it too is a first principle; but in it intellect also itself resides by reason of its being still more general. 'I am the ruler [and I will such developments for my own enjoyment,'—this is the utterance of Egoism;] and since all things are thus created by volition and are determined by Egoism, Egoism is the cause of the subtil elements, the gross elements, and the organs of sense and action; but among these also we must likewise allow that the respective genera, called the several 'forms'[3] of sound, touch, form, taste, and smell, are likewise themselves the causes of their respective grosser developments [ether, air, etc.]. If you object,[4] that "if this were the case, we should be able to detect these first

intelligence,—these two pervade the jar; by the first ignorance is destroyed, from the manifestation the jar itself bursts forth into view.') We must here take the latter sense, as we must consider *buddhi* to be directly illumined by the manifestation of intelligence (which is called 'the witness' in the text); but even so this would contradict the true notion of *buddhi*, as it is not a proper object for itself to cognise [just as the eye cannot see itself],—and therefore it is not the true material cause of the world." I read in p. 63, line 9, बुद्धितत्त्वव्यभिचारो for -व्यभिचारि, but one of the Sansk. Coll. MSS. reads the lines very differently from the printed text, बुद्धेस्तु साक्षिभास्याया बोद्धव्यत्वं यतो धियः। बोद्धव्याया बुद्धिजत्वे व्यभिचारोऽपि संभवेत्॥

1 Having spoken of creation, the writer proceeds to describe the order in which it proceeds.

2 Chhándogya Upanishad, vi. 2.

3 Scil. *śabdatwa*, etc.

4 This is said to a Naiyáyika objector.

principles everywhere"—I answer that I quite allow it, since in fact we do perceive these underlying first principles, when we once recognise their developments, in exactly the same way as you recognise your genera in the different individuals.[1] Such is the progressive expansion of the 'general' first principles as developed in the 'special' ones; and the fact is undoubted that all the first principles, beginning with Brahman, combine to be the material cause of every material product, as *e.g.* yonder pot.

Nor would it be right to object that our first principles are superfluous as causes, because it is sufficient to assume pre-existing desert[2] as the one necessary cause of everything in the world;—for nothing can ever be made without its being identical with its material cause, and your pre-existing desert [being only the instrumental cause] cannot produce this identity.[3]

Moreover, these first principles, which are the causes of the world, are also indirectly means to Liberation;[4] therefore, since individual souls are multitudinous and not identical,[5] intellect, egoism, etc., have been created separately in the case of each individual.[6] Intellect never wholly ceases from the first creation in an æon to the final destruction; but individual intellects are temporarily abolished during sound sleep, and this abolition is unending in Liberation.

But the creation of all things in succession from Intellect,

1 The follower of the Nyáya recognises one genus *aśwatwa* (the εἶδος of horse) in all individual horses,—so we recognise the features of intellect, egoism, etc., in all the different products which make up the world around and in us.

2 *Karman.*

3 The Paṇḍit explains śl. 13*b* (*tádátmyád anthathá 'siddheḥ*) as *tádátmyaṃ viná vastuno 'sambhavát* (*i.e.* the *anyathásiddhi* of l. *a* is the well-known technical term, in l. *b* it is to be resolved into two words). The 'pre-existent desert' is an *instrumental*, not a *material*, cause; and its presence has nothing to do with the necessary relations between the material cause and its effect.

4 Intellect, egoism, etc. (since life is impossible without them), contribute to produce that knowledge of and faith in God which produce Liberation.

5 *i.e.* so far as their phenomenal (*vyávahárika*) nature is concerned.

6 I understand *práṇinám* before *atádátmyát*.

as held by the atheistic Sánkhyas, is untenable, from the absence of any proof to uphold it,—this is declared in the next Aphorism.

[Creation] is not from the individual intellects because it is impossible. (88).

From whose intellect is the successive creation of gods, ṛishis, etc., declared in the Veda to have been produced? This creation is not possible;[1] therefore there must be a Supreme intelligent Lord.

Having created high and low he also creates the Vedas like a father. (89).

Having created all beings high and low, according to their respective merits and demerits, He creates the Vedas through His desire for their welfare. As a father, having begotten children, teaches them also by his words the unknown means of attaining good and avoiding evil, so does He too, this supreme Lord.

If you say 'Not so, from the mixed teaching,' we reply No, from the extreme smallness [of the part which you object to]. (90).

If you object, "But this Lord is not benevolent like a father, since his teachings relate to sacrifices which are mixed up with injurious acts productive of sin;"[2]—we answer, No, for, inasmuch as the [evil] fruit of these injurious accessory parts is so small in comparison with the bliss produced by the principal parts, the enjoiner of the former is not to be accounted therefrom other than benevolent.—"But should we not rather say, that, since the injurious act (which is only an ancillary portion) has no fruit of its own apart from the general result of the whole sacrifice, the general prohibition

[1] As I cannot translate the reading *sambhavád bhútasargo 'yam*, I adopt the reading of the Sanskrit Coll. MS. *na sambhavati sargo 'yam*.

[2] This alludes to the slaying of animals enjoined in so many of the ceremonial sacrifices.

['thou shalt not harm living things'] has no force in reference to such enjoined ancillary acts; otherwise there would be simultaneously one command to perform and another to abstain from performing, and consequently there would be an option left to the sacrificer; therefore the general prohibition only holds in those cases where there is no special injunction to suspend it, just as we see in the general injunction regarding the offering in the A'havaníya fire."[1] To this we reply,—we grant that injury to living beings produces an evil desert so far as it goes, and that all such injury is a cause of sin; here there is no dispute between us.

"But if this be so," our opponent replies, "then,—as the meaning of an 'injunction' really is that it will produce a desired end unaccompanied by any predominant undesirable result,[2]—this general injunction, as it is accompanied by a 'not,' ['thou shalt not harm living things'] warns us that this characteristic is absent from such actions, and thus all this injury to living beings [in sacrifices] produces sin and misery[3]

[1] This púrvapaksha expresses the doctrine of the Nyáya and Mímáṃsá schools, and shows how they meet the objection against the Veda drawn from the killing of animals enjoined in the sacrifices. They hold that an ancillary part of a rite has no fruit of its own apart from the general fruit of the whole,—it only exists for that whole; consequently it does not come within the scope of the general prohibition, as this only refers to independent acts.—The allusion to the A'havaníya fire is to be explained as follows. It is said in the Taittiríya Bráhmaṇa (i. 1. 10. 6), "whatever he offers in the A'havaníya fire, therewith is the fire worshipped and pleased by him," the A'havaníya fire is therefore that in which the offerings of butter, etc., called *áhutis*, are generally offered. Now in the offering connected with the ceremony called *upanayana* (when a father takes his son to the teacher), it is said that three *áhutis* are to be offered; but these are not to be offered in the consecrated A'havaníya fire but in unconsecrated, as the boy, having as yet no learning, has as yet no right to the A'havaníya, see Jaiminíya-nyáya-málá-vistara, vi. 8. 2. Here therefore the general rule is suspended by the special rule which is only an ancillary part of the *upanayana.*

[2] This is the view of the modern Nyáya, see Siddhánta Muktávalí, p. 135. (Cf. Kusumánjali, transl. p. 80.)

[3] There is an important misprint in p. 65, l. 14; दुःखाद्यहेतुता should be दुखाघहेतुता, which is the reading of the Sansk. Coll. and the Oxford MSS. The Sansk. Coll. MSS. read the whole line,

तथा सर्वात्महिंसाया अस्या दुःखाघहेतुता,

which I have adopted in the above translation.

[and consequently all such actions are to be scrupulously avoided]."

We grant all this to a certain extent; but the pain, which arises as an ancillary part of a sacrifice, is not 'predominant,' since it is inseparably connected[1] [as a preliminary] with that happiness of heaven, etc., which is the fruit of the sacrifice as a whole. Otherwise if we did not analyse this notion of 'predominance' [but allowed all kinds of pain to be *ipso facto* 'predominant'], we should have to extend the deterring influence of pain too far, [and exclude all action of every kind, through a dread of some minor pain inseparably connected with it;] therefore this idea of 'predominance,' as applied to pain, is a special characteristic[2] [whose presence or absence can only be inferred in each case from the result]. Thus, for instance, in the case of death as an expiation for some heinous guilt or in that of suicide at the meeting of the rivers at Prayága, the pain of self-destruction is light compared with the benefit resulting from the act, [but not so in the case of a slight toothache or fever]. Hence Panchaśikha has said that this pain is 'to be borne with patience,' from its being so small; but it is not so to be borne where it assumes a real importance from being predominant.[3]

[We also find expiatory rites provided to meet this necessary killing of animals, for] there are general rules declared by the Veda, enjoining the performance of the Paryagni rite;[4] while

[1] Just as the hungry man will still gladly eat, in spite of the trouble of obtaining, cooking, and lifting up his food to his mouth, which are inseparable adjuncts.

[2] *Játiviśesha* seems here to mean much the same as our 'differentia,' *i.e.* it forms a class.

[3] This refers to a sútra of Panchaśikha (an ancient teacher of the Sánkhya said to have been a disciple of Kapila's pupil, Ásuri), quoted in Vyása's Comment. to the Yoga Sútras, ii. 13, and in Váchaspati's Tattwa-Kaumudí (Kár. 2), "the mixture with a very small pain is easy to be obviated [by expiations], and to be borne with patience, and it is not enough to destroy one's merits. Why so? Because I have much other merit stored up, in which this little annoyance being thrown will make little diminution in heaven."

[4] "The priest takes a firebrand from the Áhavaníya fire and carries it on the right side thrice round the animal which is to be sacrificed."—Haug, Ait. Bráhm. transl. ii. 5. This rite is to avert evil, see Taitt. Bráhm. ii. 1. 3.

Manu provides for the five slaughter-places in the householder's house.[1] Since then we have here no principle of universal applicability [but one strictly limited to the duly initiated Vedic householder and priest,] and since it will apply still less to one who is devoid of the due qualifications, to whom shall the player who presumes to slaughter animals fly for refuge?[2]

But since from their connexion with Śruti, these śruti-ordained rites produce desert [and consequent fruit,] then the question arises, does that desert [and fruit] belong to the performer or the enjoyer, or does it reside in the Supreme Lord?

Bádaráyaṇa says[3] *that the fruit comes from Him, because we see it is so in ordinary life.* (91).

We see in common life that the ordinary rewards and punishments of men's actions come from the king's being pleased or displeased; and the Saint Bádaráyaṇa declares that they similarly come from Him, Brahman.

The fruit does not reside in the doer, because we see that, when the father performs the ordained rite on the birth of a son, it is the son [not the father] who receives the fruit [in the shape of ceremonial purity, health, etc.]. If you maintain that the enjoyment of the fruit resides in the enjoyer, we must still discuss where it really resides,—for yours will be only a tautological definition, since each term will depend on the other for its being intelligible.[4] Therefore from the analogy of ordinary life, we conclude that it is from the Supreme Lord's being pleased or displeased, that a good or an evil result arrives to the

[1] Manu, iii. 68, 69. These five 'slaughter-places,' *i.e.* the fireplace, the grindstone, the broom, the mortar, and the waterjar, are only expiated by the five daily sacrifices.

[2] In the Vishṇu Pur. ii. 6. 21, it is said that "players, fishermen, poisoners, informers, etc., will go to hell,"—the player is therefore by his profession at once debarred from offering sacrifice. I follow the Sansk. Coll. MSS. and read **नरः कं** for **नरकं**.

[3] Vedánta Sútras, iii. 2. 38.

[4] *i.e.* if you are asked where the enjoyment resides, you answer 'in the enjoyer;' if you are asked who the enjoyer is, you answer 'he who possesses the enjoyment.' (I read in l. 15 *savyapekshaṇát.*)

person who is its proper subject. Nor need we assume any intermediate link to account for the fact of the results thus gravitating to the proper subject [*i.e.* we need not bring in a new influence of *apúrva* or desert to explain it]; else we should have to bring in the same idea of *apúrva* in ordinary life, in the case of the service or offence done to the king [and the consequent reward or punishment]. Hence it is that we find it expressly stated in the Śruti[1] that human actions give pleasure to I'śwara.

"But they who follow out this ambrosial doctrine as I have declared it, full of faith and devoted to me, they my votaries are exceedingly dear to me."

And although we thus ascribe to Him displeasure and pleasure, the Supreme Lord is not thereby brought within the sphere of phenomenal life, for He himself is all that exists, He is exempt from all pain, and He is likewise eternally free.

Dissolution arises from a regression, for so it is seen to be. (92).

Dissolution [as in the great periodical mundane destructions] is held to arise from a regression of 'the special' elements into 'the general,'[2] since we see, by actual observation, that the special forms, as *e.g.*, jars, etc., are resolved into the general substance earth.

Here ends the first daily portion of the third chapter of the Commentary on the hundred Aphorisms of Śáṇḍilya composed by the most learned teacher Swapneśwara.

The second daily Portion.

The individual soul's becoming one with Brahman is called Liberation; by accurately discussing this the nature of the one great object of Faith will also be made more clear. While investigating the question 'how can one thing become another?' the author of the Aphorisms declares the capability of the individual souls to become Bhagavat.

[1] Bhagavad-gítá, xii. 20.
[2] Cf. the beginning of the Comm. on Aph. 87, and my note on Aph. 48.

Its unity appears as diversity or unity, according to the influence or the destruction of the disguiser, as is the case with the sun. (93).

It is said in the Chhándogya Upanishad (iii. 14), "All this is verily Brahman," and in the Kaṭha (iv. 11), "There is here no variety whatever;" and so also in such passages of the Gítá as these (xiii. 32 and 2),

"As the one sun illumines all this world, so, O son of Bharata, the soul illumines all the body;"

"And know me also, O son of Bharata, to be the embodied soul in all bodies,"

the soul's nature is expressly declared to be unity; therefore the idea of diversity which presents itself apparently to consciousness, really belongs to the internal organ as the disguiser and is produced by it in the soul.[1] And so too says the Śruti, "It is seen in one way and likewise in many ways, as the moon in water;" and so again (in the Vishṇu Puráṇa, II. xvi. 22),

"As the one sky is apparently seen diversified as white, blue, etc., so Soul, which is in truth but one, is seen by those of confused vision as distinct in different persons."

When by the highest form of faith, the internal organ, which is the soul's disguiser, is destroyed, this essential oneness comes out without any contradiction, just as is the case with the sun, whose nature is light, as soon as its reflecting disguisers, as mirrors, etc., are destroyed.[2]

If you say 'Souls are distinct,'—not so,—because as self-manifesting light they would have no connexion with the Supreme Soul.[3] (94).

Some hold that "souls are several, entirely distinct from each other, each consisting of self-manifesting light; for otherwise

[1] In p. 65, last l. and p. 66, line 1, the Sansk. Coll. MS. has a much more intelligible reading than that given in the printed text उभयथा — अनुष्ठत:, which I have adopted. It is as follows,

अत एव यो नानात्वप्रत्ययः स जीवोपाधिबुद्धेरात्मनि क्षतः।

[2] The individual soul is the reflection of Soul on the mirroring internal organ (*taijasa*).

[3] The Sansk. Coll. MS. reads *prakáśátmanám* for *prakáśánam.*

you could not say that such a soul was liberated and such a soul bound;" but this opinion must be rejected, for even if it might be consistently held by the atheistic Sánkhyas, it certainly cannot by the Theistic Sánkhyas [and much less by us Vedántins]. How so? Because, consisting as they do of self-manifesting light, there could be no such a relation between the Supreme Soul and them as seer and object seen, since they would not be illumined by him, just as lamps, as self-manifesting, are not illumined by the sun. And hence we should have to admit in Brahman an absence of omnipotence and omniscience, and the consequent capability of being himself knowable [as not himself infinite]. Nor yet[1] can we allow that souls are illumined [by Brahman],—because it would follow from this that they were themselves non-intelligent.[2] Nor can we allow that souls are illumined [and thus manifested] by the mutual evolution of their internal organs; because this manifestation is produced by the removal of the darkness [which veiled the otherwise self-revealing object],[3] and not by the evolution

[1] The Sansk. Coll. MS. reads in p. 68, l. 16, न च प्रकाश्याः; if we read अथ we must suppose न to be omitted (cf. note *suprà*, p. 67).

[2] There is a rule यद्धि परस्य प्रकाश्यं तज्जडम्.

[3] This passage is only cleared up by a comparison with the statement in p. 72, ll. 13, 14 (Calc. text), see *infrà*, p. 108. The author seems in both to diverge slightly from the usual Vedánta doctrine. He holds that by the connexion of the senses with an external object, the darkness of ignorance which previously concealed that object from the internal organ is removed; then that form of the internal organ called the understanding (*buddhi*), influenced by the quality of 'goodness,' becomes evolved so as to assume the form of that object, and is illumined by the light of Brahman; and by that light the object is thus rendered manifest. Thus the eye of a certain man comes in contact with a jar, and the ignorance which had concealed that jar from him is removed; his understanding next assumes the form of the jar, and is illumined by the light of Brahman, and the jar is made visible to that individual. (In the Vedántasára the understanding itself removes the ignorance by its evolution (*vṛitti*), while here the connexion of the senses removes the ignorance or darkness, and the understanding is subsequently evolved and illumined.) In the supposed case where one individual soul makes another soul its object (as also in that where the soul makes Brahman its object), the former step alone is possible, as the object, being self-luminous, shows itself as soon as the intervening obstacles are removed. (Cf. Vedánta S. pp. 22, 23.) One of the Sansk. Coll. MSS. reads l. 17 *tamo 'bhibhútyaivántaḥkaraṇasattwavṛittyá*, which seems an attempt to bring the statement in harmony with the usual doctrine; but cf. p. 72 (Calc. text).

of the internal organ under the predominance of the quality of goodness [which causes it to cognise].

This manifestation [by the evolution of the understanding] is out of the question, as in this case it is wholly inapplicable [since the soul is essentially light, and will therefore show itself]. For we see also in the external world that, even though the veil between two lamps [caused by a curtain] is removed, one lamp cannot be illumined by the other [since both are self-luminous].

Thus we learn that in the case of the external and internal light [*i.e.* the lamp and the soul,—however different in other respects they may be from each other], there is found a common though non-essential quality,[1] [*i.e.* their incapability of being illumined by anything else]; and it is the presence of this common quality which enables us to apply the word 'light' [properly applicable only to the external object] to the soul in a metonymical sense based on likeness,[2] as in those words of the Bṛihad Áraṇyaka Upanishad, iv. 3. 9, "this soul becomes itself pure light."

Therefore the soul which is pure thought is proved to exist solely by the very fact of its illumining the world [and thus making it an object of cognition]; no external proof is needed. And again, the existence of soul is incontestably established by the fact that it is the receptacle of those attributes of the internal organ which are erroneously reflected on it, and that it is also the only site of all essential knowledge; while we can only apply the terms 'knowledge' and 'happiness' in a secondary and figurative sense to the functions of the understanding.

"What proof can there possibly be of the existence of

[1] An *aupádhika dharma* is one which does not arise from a thing's nature but from some external relation between it and something else,—it is nearly equal to our 'accidental.'

[2] Cf. Sáhitya Darpaṇa, pp. 14, 15. A metonymical meaning (*lakshya*) is called *gauṇa* when it is based on likeness, as when we say 'that ass the man from the Punjab,' not meaning that the man is actually a quadruped, but that he resembles the ass in stupidity and obstinacy.

separate souls? That the primary principle, the 'understanding' (*buddhi*), exists separately [as associated with separate individual personalities] is certain enough; how otherwise could there be the determination of bondage or freedom in the case of souls which in themselves are eternally free?"[1]

"Well then, let souls[2] be capable of being modified, and let knowledge, desire, etc., be their qualities, from the fact that we are conscious of such perceptions as 'I know,' 'I desire,' 'I am happy,' etc." The author refutes this opinion in the following aphorism.

Souls, however, are not capable of modifications, because it is the instrument which is modified. (95).

Souls are not capable of such modifications as knowledge, etc.; why? because knowledge, etc., are accounted for by the fact that the perception of pleasure, etc., belongs to the instrument [*i.e.* the mind], and consequently the souls are unmodified. Thus in the inference [already given in p. 3] "the perception of pleasure is through an instrument," we assume that the connexion[3] between the perception and the instrument is that of identity;[4] and again there is also the argument "pleasure, etc., are not modifications of soul, because they are perceived [as reflected] in soul, as paleness, etc., are perceived [as reflected] in soul."[5] So too the mind perceives the idea of self, by being identical with its cause [egoism]; and consequently, as the mind itself is dissolved during sound sleep, we have in sound sleep no self-consciousness. Moreover, these apparent qualities of mind [*i.e.* joy, knowledge, etc.] are really what

[1] This answers the difficulty suggested *suprà*.

[2] In p. 69, l. 6, I read with the Sansk. Coll. MS. *santu átmánaḥ* for *sattátmánaḥ*.

[3] The Sansk. Coll. MS. and the Oxford MS. read in p. 69, l. 12, °करणसंबन्धस्य.

[4] *i.e.* joy, knowledge, etc., really reside in and constitute the internal organ, but are only reflected in soul. In p. 72 (Calc. ed.) they are called *buddher vikáráḥ*.

[5] This refers to such expressions as "I am pale, etc.," where the quality which really belongs to the body is reflected on the soul and applied to it. Cf. *suprà*, p. 3.

constitute mind, just as the so-called limitations of time[1] are really what constitute time itself. This short discussion will suffice for our purpose here.

He next proceeds to discuss how the soul becomes Brahman.

This is produced through the absolute abolition of the individual's understanding[2] *by undeviating faith.* (96).

It is said [in the Gítá (viii. 22)],

"He is that supreme spirit, O son of Prithá, who is to be attained by undeviating faith, in whom all beings reside and by whom all this world was spread out." And so also [in the Nṛisiṃha-puráṇa], "Wherefore is not an effort made for liberation into the ancient spirit, who is to be attained only by faith?" Therefore Liberation is the attainment of the joy of Brahman, when the individual understanding is entirely abolished by the highest faith,—this is the true meaning. And therefore its definition is in fact declared to be the attainment of that joy of Brahman unaccompanied by the antecedent non-existence of the abolition of the individual understanding.[3] (Here we consider the 'understanding' (*buddhi*) as the disguiser of the individual soul [and not really belonging to it], since we only accept the understanding as belonging to God[4] [all creation being produced by his Máyá].)

If you rejoin, that "by this last view of yours the attainment

[1] The Nyáya holds that although time is in itself only one, it is called by the names moment, day, month, etc., past, present and future, through different limitations or accidental conditions (*upádhi*). Thus that time is called 'past' which is the counter-entity of a present 'emergent non-existence,' as the past day; that time is called 'future' which is the counter-entity of a present 'antecedent non-existence,' as the following day; that time is called 'present' which is at once the counter-entity of a past 'antecedent non-existence' and of a coming 'emergent non-existence.'

[2] Sc. *buddhi.*—In Aph. 96 I read with Sansk. Coll. MS. *tadbuddhilayát* for *tadbuddhir buddhilâyát.*

[3] In p. 70, l. 4, I read with the Sansk. Coll. MS. *prágabhávásahavṛitti.* If we read with the printed text *sahavṛitti,* I suppose it must mean that the soul *really* existed in Brahman, even before the understanding (*buddhi*) associated with it was abolished,—although of course it was not conscious of it through the delusion produced by that association.

[4] I follow the Sansk. Coll. MS. in reading line 7 of p. 70 here, after *súchitam.* It is separated from its context as given in the printed text.

of the joy of Brahman would no longer be an end for man, as it is not really a future thing to be attained, but one already possessed and settled [the soul being even now identical with Brahman];"—we reply that it is still an object for man to pursue, as it also admits of being determined by a special relation to himself, just as a village may be [for although the village already exists and is not to be produced by our will, we can still produce by our efforts a direct relation between us and it as proprietors and property]. Otherwise [if you absolutely denied that what is thus determined by something else can be an object for man, even though from another point of view it is not fixed,] it would follow that even happiness itself could not be an object for man. For we cognise it as the thing 'happiness' (*sukha*) determined by the general idea of happiness (*sukhatwa*) which inheres in it, and this general idea [like all *játis*] is eternal and therefore fixed; and therefore our wishes and volitions would have no power to pursue it, as these [unlike the power of cognition] cannot separate the determined from the determinant.[1] Therefore we maintain that wish and volition, under the colour of that part of the object which is unfixed, pursue also that which is fixed, both being to them inseparably united.[2] If you say that the knowledge that the object is not to be attained by our volition will always act as a restraint,—we reply that there is no incongruity in supposing that a violent passion may lead irresistibly to action by overshadowing the idea that the desired end is

[1] The Hindus hold that on the contact of the organ of sense with an object, as *e.g.* a jar, there arises the idea of a jar and also the idea of the nature, *i.e.* εἶδος, of jar (both being equally objects of perception) but the two ideas are distinct,—this is *nirvikalpaka*. Subsequently the mind combines them into one idea, 'a jar possessing the species or nature of jar,' and this is *savikalpaka*. We are however not conscious of the first step,—it is only recognised as necessary from an analysis of the subsequent compound idea. Swapneśwara maintains that 'wish' and 'volition' have not this double mode of exercise which the power of cognition has; they can only act as *sa-vikalpaka* and seize the desired object together with its species, *i.e.* they cannot separate the non-eternal individual pleasure from the eternal and fixed species or general idea residing in it.

[2] In p. 70, l. 10, read with the Oxford and Sanskrit Coll. MSS. सिद्धेऽपीहाश्नती.

not wholly attainable by our volition,—just as in the parallel case of the hawk-sacrifice,[1] where anger overshadows the knowledge in the sacrificer's mind that it will be accompanied by a predominant undesirable result[2] [*i.e.* hell].

Moreover it is said in an A'gama, "Joy is the essential character of Brahman, and that becomes present in liberation," and this very text proves that the attaining of such a state is an object to be striven for.

"But even if this supreme faith be established,—just as the pre-existing merit and demerit which produce the necessity of living in the present life can only be abolished by experiencing these effects, so too the other forms of merit and demerit can be similarly cancelled only by experience; and hence there can be no such thing as final liberation after all." To this objection he replies,

So long as life lasts in the one case; but the others will be cancelled from the absence of any place for them to abide in. (97).

When this devotion to the supreme soul is produced, the words of the Chhándogya Upanishad come true,[3] (vi. 14),

"So long it [bodily existence] remains to him, until he shall be liberated [from merit or demerit]; then he shall attain to the end."

And so too in the Vishṇu Puráṇa (I. ii. 20),

"What has he to do with merit, wealth or desire? Liberation is placed in his grasp, who has firm faith in thee, the root of all worlds."

By 'life' is meant the merit which operates to produce life in this present birth; this, so long as it lasts, hinders liberation even though the highest faith exists,—so long the devotee only attains *jívan-mukti.*[4] But since, when the merit which produces

1 "Let him who desires to kill his enemy by incantation offer the hawk-sacrifice." —Shaḍviṃśa Br. iii. 8.

2 Cf. Kusumánjali, v. 13.

3 Compare the similar argument in S'ankara's Commentary on this passage of the Upanishad.

4 "The third kind of liberation is effectual in lifetime (*jívan-mukti*) and enables he possessor of it to perform supernatural actions; as evocation of shades of progeni-

life is cancelled, the understanding also entirely ceases, the 'other' merits and demerits will also be 'cancelled,' *i.e.* will not produce experience,[1] from the absence of any place for this to abide in.[2] Hence it does not follow, as you supposed, that there can be no such thing as final liberation,—since even the understanding itself acts negatively as one of its causes, by the very fact that it can be so changed [*i.e.* can be cancelled, and therefore cease to hinder the desired issue]. Nor need we suppose that these other merits and demerits will in this view cease altogether to be causes; because a cause does not altogether cease to be a cause, because its necessary concurrent is not present.[3]

[An objector might however say that "merit and demerit (which constitute fate or *adṛishṭa*) might be thus cancelled, if they resided in the intellect of the person to whom they belong; but you hold that they reside in the intellect of the Supreme Lord, for you declared in your Commentary on the 91st Aphorism that our rewards and punishments came from Brahman's being pleased or displeased; and therefore, as residing in Him, they cannot be thus cancelled." We reply,] This *adṛishṭa* which resides in the mind of the Supreme Lord in the form of his pleasure or displeasure can be cancelled by the effect of time or by the occurrence of a mundane catastrophe, just as the effects of the several parts of a sacrifice, which are being accumulated towards the aggregated total, may be cancelled by the failure of one part, and thus fail to produce the general effect.[4] The transference of

tors, etc., translation of himself into other bodies called into existence by the mere force of his will, etc."—Colebrooke, Essays, vol. i. p. 399.

[1] In p. 7i, line 4, read with the Sanskrit Coll. MS. भोगास्पदस्याभावाद्धानि-र्भोगाभाव एवेति. The printed text seems to me meaningless.

[2] *Buddhi* being the site of all phenomenal consciousness.

[3] *i.e.* the gunpowder still retains its power of causing an explosion, though without the concurrence of a spark it will not actually exercise it.

[4] The new-moon and full-moon sacrifices consist of six parts, as the offering to Agni, etc.; each of these parts produces its own partial adṛishṭa; but the general adṛishṭa is only produced by the united effect of all. If a sacrificer had completed five of these partial offerings and died before the completion of the sixth, the general effect would be lost.

all the result of our actions to the Supreme Being [which our theory so earnestly inculcates] directly abolishes the tendency of these 'hindering' actions to produce bondage. The fire of knowledge only destroys the influence of our actions *indirectly* [by leading to faith; but not *directly*, as Śankara's followers would inculcate].

Their mundane existence arises from want of faith, not from ignorance, since this is not established to be a cause.[1] (98).

"Is the mundane existence of the individual soul considered to be caused by ignorance, or is it caused by want of faith?" The Aphorism proceeds to answer this question.—A temporary heaven,—liberation while still alive,—and absolute liberation,—these are the three paths; liberation while still alive implies the possession of the highest faith; but the want thereof involves a mundane course from birth to birth. This mundane existence arises from the absence of the desire of faith; when faith is produced, it ceases; and thus has it been said by the great sages;

"So long are there pain and this desire, so long infatuation and sorrow, while the soul does not fly for refuge to thee, the deliverer from all sin" (Vishṇu Puráṇa, I. ix. 72).[2]

The creation is caused by ignorance of the truth; by knowledge we hold that creation is abolished; when the causes vanish which produce the snake and the rope, these effects likewise cease to exist. The succession of births, the dreadful scourgings of Yama's attendants, the various sufferings, and the sight of the Son of the Sun (Yama),—these are the mirage of the wave of the creature's egoism and personality;—the effect of turning away from the lotus of Krishṇa's feet.

They have three eyes, like Rudra, divided as revealed speech, a sign, and sense-perception. (99).

'They,' *i.e.* embodied souls, have 'three eyes,' *i.e.* three means

[1] The Sansk. Coll. MS. reads *abhakteḥ* and *kdraṇatwdsiddheḥ*, but both are rather glosses than the true reading.

[2] For तु सा the Bombay edition of the Vishṇu P. reads तथा.

or 'proofs' for attaining certain knowledge of things. Although they do not differ as to being certain, they are three as being three different instruments. Thus 'speech' [*i.e.* Revelation] produces verbal certainty, being in the form of certain words and their meanings which are congruous and understood. Revelation is here mentioned first [and not, as is usual, sense-perception,] in order to declare its pre-eminent efficiency as a means for producing supernatural faith. So again the knowledge of 'a sign' [or middle term] which abides in the minor term and is invariably accompanied by a known major term, is the cause of inferential certainty; and in our school we should not dispute the definition, if [instead of the words 'the knowledge of a sign which abides in the minor term, etc.,'] it ran 'the sign when recognised as abiding, etc.,' for we hold that an effect always exists in its cause.[1] Again, the senses when in contact with their objects are the causes of certain perceptive knowledge; and these are six, the organs of smell, taste, sight, touch, hearing, and the mind [or the perceptive power]; and these, by their connexion with their objects, having overpowered the darkness of ignorance which had enveloped the internal organ,[2] produce an evolution of it as influenced by the quality of goodness, so that it forthwith assumes the form of the object as illumined by the light of the Brahma-soul. Hence it is said in the Gítá (xiv. 11),

"Light arises in this body through all its avenues."

But when we say that joy, sorrow, etc., are also perceived [as well as external objects], and speak of them as modifications of the understanding[3] which is associated with the individual soul,—it must be remembered that these

[1] If we said that 'a sign, when recognised as abiding in the minor term, etc., is the cause of an inference,' it might be objected that in this case no inference could be drawn if the sign were past or future at the time of inferring (see *Bhásháparichchheda*, śl. 66). He replies that in his view (as in that of the Sánkhyas) an effect is always existing in its cause, and therefore the sign will still be equally present, though latent.

[2] Compare with this my note, *suprà*, p. 100.

[3] *Buddhi.*

are made manifest by the soul's own immediate light; and we have no need to assume the process of an evolution of the quality of goodness in the understanding to account for their being perceived,—since it would be uselessly cumbrous. These in truth are to be illumined by the witness Soul directly. There are therefore only three proofs, revealed speech, inference, and sense-perception, like the three organs of sight in Rudra, neither more nor less,—and like them they imply an identity with the moon, the sun, and fire.[1] The supposed proof called Comparison is only useful for comprehending the direct meaning of a word; and this is effected by the mind with the assistance of the 'analogous'[2] form of inference, starting from the recognised fact that a well-known word is applied to the same object to which the unknown word is applied [as in the stock instance that '*a bos gavæus* means an animal like a cow,'][3] just as we determine by analogy the metaphorical meanings of the words and phrases of poetry.[4] 'Comparison' is therefore included in the three above-mentioned proofs and is not required as a separate one. We do not extend this discussion on the different proofs any further here, as it has been fully discussed by us in the 'Touchstone of the first principles of the Nyáya,' and in the 'Touchstone of the first principles of the Vedánta.'[5]

1 S'iva's right eye is the sun, his left is the moon, and his third eye in the centre of his forehead is fire. I suppose that the sun properly stands for revelation as being the brightest, the moon for inference (from its connexion with *paksha* as 'the lunar fortnight' and 'the minor term,') and the five fires for the five senses. In the text, however, the moon is put first in the compound (according to the rule *abhyarhitaṃ cha*) as being the monarch of the stars, planets, and bráhmans, see Vishṇu Pur. I. xxii.

2 For the *sámányato dṛishṭa* form of inference see Nyáya Sútras, i. 5,—it is where the inference is drawn from generic qualities, the specific ones being unnoticed, as 'it is a substance because it has the nature of earth.' The 'sign' is not here the cause or the effect, as in the *púrvavat* or *s'eshavat* form.

3 This is contrary to the Nyáya as well as the Vedánta, both of which accept Comparison (*upamána*) as a proof. Cf. my notes to the Kusumánjali, translation, iii. sections 10–12.

4 Or this might mean, "just as we determine the meaning of the word 'section as applied to poetry."

5 I know nothing of these two works; neither is mentioned in Dr. Hall's Bibliographical Index.

The 'intellect'[1] [or 'understanding'] associated with the individual soul is the same as the 'mind';[2] this faculty possesses the power of contraction and expansion; and in this way we account for the simultaneousness and non-simultaneousness of perceptions.[3]

Since the intellects thus associated with the individual souls sprang from the egoism of Íśwara [or Brahmá], the idea of 'I' is grasped directly [without any action of the perceptive faculty or any evolution of the intellect itself[4]] as residing in the intellect, just like pain, pleasure, etc.[5]

Again, since the subtil elements, the gross elements, the organs of sensation and action, etc., were produced by the intellect of Íśwara, all this [external world] is to be known by Íśwara's intellect,[6]—it can therefore be grasped by the soul and by its associated senses.[7]

[1] Here follows a digression on 'perception.'

[2] The Sánkhya considers 'intellect,' 'egoism,' and 'mind' as quite distinct from each other; the Vedánta holds that the internal organ has a fourfold division from its different modifications. Thus understanding or intellect (*buddhi*) is that modification of the internal organ which consists in assurance; mind (*manas*), that which consists in resolution or irresolution; thought (*chitta*), that which consists in investigation; and egoism (*ahaṃkára*), that which consists in self-consciousness. See Vedánta-sára, p. 8.

[3] According to the Sánkhya two or more perceptions may be simultaneous, as the smelling, seeing and touching of a flower,—according to the Nyáya they are successive, as the mind, being *atomic*, can only receive one sensation at a time,—the apparent simultaneousness is only caused by very rapid succession, like the apparent circle of light caused by a rapidly whirled torch. Our author maintains that the mind, which he here identifies with the intellect (*buddhi*), is not atomic but susceptible of expansion and of contraction, and when it is thus expanded it can receive several sensations at the same time, when contracted it can only receive one.

[4] Cf. *suprà*, p. 100 and p. 109.

[5] The Sánkhya and Vedánta hold that pain, pleasure, etc., are qualities which reside in the intellect but are reflected upon soul, and so wrongly attributed to it; the Nyáya of course calls them qualities of soul.

[6] The paṇḍit quotes a *niyama* or principle, यदस्य बुद्ध्या क्रियते तत् तस्य बुद्धिवेद्यं भवत्येव.

[7] This passage is very obscure. I can only suppose that it means that our intellects having sprung from Íśwara's egoism, must be capable of being connected with the external world which was produced by his intellect (see p. 91). The process by which it is known is that before described; the senses remove the darkness, and our intellect, being evolved so as to assume the shape of the object, is then illumined by the soul's light. (The subtil elements are only perceptible to yogins.)

The five gross elements, the five subtil elements, the eleven organs [of sense and action], egoism, intellect, Nature, the soul and the Supreme Lord—these form the aggregate of the twenty-six first principles.

Manifestation[1] *and disappearance are changes [of the existing], from the connexion with the result of the action expressed by the verb.* (100).

The author proceeds to discuss a mundane creation and destruction, as being collaterally related to the subject. Now creation is defined as a 'manifestation,' *i.e.* the competency of an already existing thing to produce its effects; while 'disappearance' is its incompetency to produce them; thus too, increase, decrease, etc., will similarly be only changes of the already existing. How so? Because in such phrases as 'he makes a pot,' 'he destroys a pot,' etc., we have a relation specified between the object and the result implied by the meaning of the root; and this relation can only take place in that which is, not in that which is not, as has been said in the Gítá (ii. 16),

> "Existence cannot belong to that which is not, nor non-existence to that which is."

So too by such phrases as 'it exists,' 'it is destroyed,' etc., we similarly understand that the subject is the site of the action implied by the root; but this power to be a site can only belong to that which is.

Now 'manifestation' [or creation] means the being connected with the initial moment [from which the subsequent series of events dates], or, as it may be more accurately defined, it is the being a counter-entity to destruction;—since our former definition was not strictly correct, as it is impossible to point out a really initial moment [as the sequence of creations and æons is eternal]. But you have no right to say that, as every manifestation must have had *its* manifestation, we must

[1] For अविस्तरो भावा read with all the MSS. आविस्तिरोभावा.

plead guilty to the faults of an '*ad infinitum* regression' or 'cumbrousness'; for the union of all the pot's antecedents (as the clay, the wheel, etc.) is really the manifestation of the pot's manifestation; and if you hesitate to grant our definition, your objections will apply with equal force to your own hypothesis of 'production,' since here too you will have to concede a similar unending succession of previous productions.[1]

And thus we may define the 'antecedent non-existence' of a pot as the succession of continued previous manifestations and disappearances, while 'destruction' [or 'emergent non-existence'] will be its 'disappearance'; and this destruction will be sometimes absolute, as in the case of the deceased Devadatta's body or of the intellects of those souls which have attained

[1] I give a translation of my paṇḍit friend's clear note on this hard passage.

'An opponent might thus argue: "But if you accept the idea of 'manifestation' and reject that of 'production,' is your 'manifestation' itself continuous or occasional? If it is continuous, why should it not be eternal? If it is occasional, then the manifestation of this said manifestation will be either continuous or occasional. But if it is continuous, you will again have to concede that it is eternal; or if it is occasional, you will have again to allow a manifestation of this occasional manifestation, and so on. Thus you will be involved in the fault of an '*ad infinitum* regression.' Or on the other hand, if, in order to avoid this fault, you allow that the second or third manifestation was produced, not manifested, you will be involved in the fault of 'cumbrousness,' because if the idea of production is to be conceded at all, it might as well be allowed at the very first step."

'We however reply:

'"We grant that if we accepted the idea that a pot's manifestation was itself manifested, and then went on to concede a further manifestation of this second manifestation, we should be involved in one of the two faults you allege; but we do not concede this. We hold indeed that the pot is manifested, not produced; but we do not allow a second separate manifestation of this manifestation,—we maintain that this manifestation of the manifestation is only another expression for the sum total of the causes which are said, in your phraseology, to produce the effect, the pot; as wherever this sum total is found, there the manifestation takes place. This explanation removes all fear of an '*ad infinitum* regression,' as there is no continued succession of supposed manifestations.

'"Nor, again, is your own hypothesis of production a whit more free from the same charge. For we may in turn ask you whether this 'production' of yours is continuous or occasional. If it is continuous, then why is it not eternal? if it is occasional, we ask whether there is a production of this production or not? and so on, thus involving either an *ad infinitum* regression, or the fault of 'cumbrousness.' And you will similarly have to assume, as we did, that the production of the first production is not something separate but is only another expression for the sum total of the causes, as in our case."'

liberation. But the so-called 'mutual non-existence' and 'absolute non-existence' are not really distinct forms of non-existence, since the former is only the possessing mutually exclusive properties, and the other is only the same as the thing's site [*i.e.* the absence of the pot really means only the spot of ground where it should have been but is not]. Otherwise, we should have to accept another absence in the first absence and so on *ad infinitum.*[1]

But in a 'mundane destruction' (*pralaya*) we have only the absence of any developments other than that particular one called a mundane destruction. But there is no difficulty in this hypothesis with regard to the arising of subsequent creations, since the latent influences produced by past acts [which are to germinate into future merit and demerit, and determine subsequent births] remain permanent in a very subtil form and are not destroyed.

Thus closes our threefold investigation into the doctrine of Faith.

May Kṛishṇa's brightness, set off by the Kaustubha gem, abide in your hearts, as he was seen clothed in yellow garments, himself dark blue like a cloud, with his long eyes like a lotus petal, holding the pipe, and adorned with the dust of the cows.[2]

[1] My paṇḍit friend thus explains this passage: "Mutual non-existence is not something distinct, but only the possession of mutually exclusive properties. Thus 'a pot is not cloth,' 'cloth is not a pot;' we have here an example of mutual non-existence. Now the pot has those qualities constituting pot-hood (*ghaṭatwa*) which are contrary to those which exist in cloth, and similarly cloth has those qualities constituting cloth-hood (*paṭatwa*) which are contrary to those which exist in a pot.—So too 'absolute non-existence' [as in the phrase 'a pot is not there'] is not something distinct, but is really the same as the *ground* where the pot is not, *i.e.* the absence of the pot is recognised in the ground [this is the Mímáṃsá doctrine, see Siddhánta-muktavalí, p. 9]. This has been accepted in order to avoid the necessity of allowing an infinite succession of absences. For as we must allow that there is no pot in the absence of a pot, we must perforce concede that there is the pot's absence in this aforesaid absence; and if this second absence be something existing by itself, a third absence of the pot will similarly have to be conceded as existing in it, and so on *ad infinitum.* Hence we maintain that the absence of a pot is not something existing by itself, but simply the spot of ground where we expected to find it and it was not there."

[2] In l. 3 the MSS. have *parimaṇḍitaṃ.*

There was in the bracelet of Bengal (*Gauḍa*), sprung from a renowned world-jewel,[1] a leader of the wise, named Viśárada, who held the post of monarch over all the rulers of the earth; from him sprang Jaleśwara, chief of the learned, and general of kings; by Swapneśa his offspring, was this investigation into the doctrine of Faith composed.

Here ends the second daily portion of the third chapter of the Commentary on the Hundred Aphorisms of Śáṇḍilya, composed by the most learned Swapneśwara, and with it ends the chapter and the book.

[1] Cf. the lines,

In earth's dark circlet once the precious gem
Of living light, O fall'n Jerusalem.

STEPHEN AUSTIN AND SONS, PRINTERS, HERTFORD.

LIST OF BOOKS FOR SALE

AT THE LIBRARY OF THE

ASIATIC SOCIETY OF BENGAL,

No. 57, PARK STREET, CALCUTTA,

AND OBTAINABLE FROM

THE SOCIETY'S LONDON AGENTS, MESSRS. TRÜBNER & CO.,
57 AND 59, LUDGATE HILL, LONDON, E. C.

BIBLIOTHECA INDICA.

Sanskrit Series.

Uttara Naishadha, 12 fasci. .... Rs.	7	8
Chaitanya-chandrodaya, Nátaka, 3 fasci.	1	14
Srauta sútra, A's'valáyana, 11 fasci.	6	14
———— Látyáyana, 9 fasci.	5	10
S'ankara-Vijaya, 3 fasci.	1	14
Vaishes'ika Darsana, 5 fasci.	3	2
Dasarúpa, 3 fasci.	1	14
Kaushitaki Bráhmanopanishad, 2 fasci.	1	4
Sánkhyasára, 1 fasci.	0	10
Brihat Sañhitá, 7 fasci.	4	6
Lalita-vistara, 6 fasci.	3	12
Taittiríya Bráhmaṇa, 24 fasci.	15	0
Taittiríya Sañhitá, 29 fasci.	18	2
Taittiríya A'raṇyaka, 11 fasci.	6	14
Maitri Upanishad, 3 fasci.	1	14
A's'valáyana Grihya Sútra, 4 fasci.	2	8
Mimáñsá Darsana, 13 fasci.	8	2
Táṇdya Bráhmaṇa, 19 fasci.	11	14
Gopatha Bráhmaṇa, 2 fasci.	1	10
Atharvana Upanishads, 5 fasci.	3	2
Agni Puráṇa, 13 fasci.	8	2
Sáma Veda Sáñhitá, 35 fasci.	21	14
Gopála Tápaní, 1 fasci.	0	10
Nrisiñha Tápaní, 3 fasci.	1	14
Chaturvarga Chintámani, 29 fasci.	18	2
Gobhilíya Grihya Sútra, 7 fasci.	4	6
Piñgala Chhandah Sútra, 3 fasci.	1	14
Taittiríya Prátis'ákhiya, 3 fasci.	1	14
Prithiráj Rásu, by Chand Bardai, 3 fasci.	1	14
Rájatarangini, ...	4	0
Mahábhárata, vols. III. and IV., ...	40	0
Purána Sangraha, ...	1	0
Páli Grammar, 2 fasci.	1	4
Aitareya Araṇyaka of the Rig Veda, 5 fasci.	3	2
Chhándogya Upanishad, English, 2 fasci.	1	4
Taittiríya, &c., Upanishads, English, 2 fasci.	1	4
Sáñkhya Aphorisms, English, 2 fasci.	1	4
Sáhitya Darpaṇa, English, 4 fasci.	2	8
Brahma Sútra, English, ...	1	0
Kátantra, 4 fasci.	4	0
Kámandakíya Nítisára, 4 fasci. (Fas. 1, out of stock.)	2	8
Bhámatí, 5 fasci.	3	2

Arabic & Persian Series.

Dictionary of Arabic Technical Terms, 20 fasci., complete, ...Rs.	25	0
Risálah-i-Shamsiyah, (Appendix to Do. Do.), ...	1	4
Fihrist Ṭúsí, 4 fasci.	3	0
Nukhbat-ul-Fikr, ...	0	10
Futúh-ul-Shám, Wáqidí, 9 fasci.	5	10
Futúh-ul-Shám, Azadí, 4 fasci.	2	8
Maghází of Wáqidí, 5 fasci.	3	2
Isábah, 28 fasci., with supplement, ...	20	14
Táríkh-i-Fíróz Sháhí, 7 fasci.	4	6
Táríkh-i-Baihaqí, complete in 9 fasci.	5	10
Muntakhab-ut-Tawáríkh, vols. I. II. and III., complete in 15 fasci.	9	6
Wís o Rámín, 5 fasci.	2	3
Iqbálnámah-i-Jahángírí, complete in 3 fasci.	1	14
'Alamgírnámah, 13 fasci., with index, ...	8	2
Pádsháhnámah, 19 fasci., with index, ...	11	14
Muntakhab-ul-Lubáb, by Kháfí Khán, 19 fasci., with index, ...	12	12
Áín-i-Akbarí, Persian text, 4to., 22 fasci.	27	8
Áín-i-Akbarí, English translation by H. Blochmann, M. A., vol. I, ...	12	4
Farhang-i-Rashídí, 14 fasci., complete, ...	17	8
Nizámí's Khiradnámah-i-Iskandarí, 2 fasci. complete, ...	2	0
Akbarnámah, 12 fasci.	15	0
Maáṣir-i-'Alamgírí, by Muhammad Ṣáqí, complete, 6 fasci., with index, ...	3	12
Haft Ásmán, history of the Persian Masnawí, ...	1	4
Ṭabaqát-i-Náçirí, English translation, by Raverty, 8 fasci.	8	0
Ṭabaqát-i-Náçirí, Persian text, 5 fasci.	3	2

MISCELLANEOUS.

Journal of the Asiatic Society of Bengal from vols. XII to XVII, 1843-48, vols. XIX to XXI, 1850-52, to Subscribers at Re. 1 per number and to non-subscribers at Re. 1-8 per number; vols. XXVI, XXVII, 1857-58, and vols. XXXIII to XLV, 1864-76, to Subscribers at 1-8 per number and to non-subscribers at Rs. 2 per number.

Asiatic Researches, vols. VII. to XII. and vols. XVII. to XX. each, ...Rs.	10	0
Do. Do. Index, ...	5	0
Catalogue of Mammalia, ...	3	0
——— of Fossil Vertebrata, ...	2	0
——— of Sanskrit Manuscripts, ...	1	0
——— of Arabic and Persian Manuscripts, ...	1	0
Tibetan Dictionary, ...	10	0
——— Grammar, ...	8	0
Ross' Annals of 'Omán, ...	2	0
Notices of Sanskrit Manuscripts, 12 fasci.	12	0
Blochmann's Persian Prosody, ...	5	0
Istiláhát-i-Súfiyah. Edited by Dr. A. Sprenger, 8vo.	1	0
Jawámi' ul-'ilm ir-riyází, 168 pages with 17 plates, 4to.	2	0
Purána Sangraha. Edited by the Rev. K. M. Banerjea, No. 1, ...	1	0
Corcoran's Chinese Empire, in Urdu, Vols. I. and II., per vol.	20	0
Aborigines of India, by B. H. Hodgson, ...	3	0
History of the Afghans, Part 1, by Dorn, ...	5	0
Examination and Analysis of the Mackenzie Manuscripts, by the Rev. W. Taylor,	2	0
Han Koong Tsew, or the Sorrows of Han, by J. Francis Davis, ...	1	8
'Ináyah, a Commentary on the Hidáyah, Vols. II. IV., ...	16	0
Analysis of the Sher Chín, by Alexander Csoma de Körös, ...	1	0
Khazánat-ul-'ilm, ...	4	0
Sharáyat-ul-Islám, ...	4	0
Anís-ul-Musharrihín, ...	3	0
Catalogue Raisonné of the Society's Sanskrit MSS. (Grammar), ...	2	0

21061400R00069

Made in the USA
Lexington, KY
10 March 2013